365 Easy Chicken Recipes

Quick, Easy Ways to Cook Chicken

Cookbook Resources LLC
Highland Village, Texas

365 Easy Chicken Recipes
Quick, Easy Ways to Cook Chicken

1st Printing - March 2008

International Standard Book No. 978-1-59769-028-7

Library of Congress No. 2008008961

Library of Congress Cataloging-in-Publication Data

     365 easy chicken recipes : quick, easy ways to cook chicken.
        p. cm.
    Includes index.
    ISBN 978-1-59769-028-7
    1. Cookery (Chicken) 2. Quick and easy cookery. I. Cookbook Resources, LLC. II. Title: Three hundred sixty-five easy chicken recipes.
    TX750.5.C45A1385 2008
    641.6'65--dc22
                      2008008961

Cover and Illustrations by Nancy Bohanan

Edited, Designed and Published in the United States of America by
Cookbook Resources, LLC
541 Doubletree Drive
Highland Village, Texas 75077

Toll free 866-229-2665

www.cookbookresources.com

cookbook
resources® LLC
Bringing Family and Friends to the Table

Easy Home
Cooking

Chicken Rules the Roost

Welcome to the world of chicken – where the bird is king and the possibilities are endless. From a succulent roasted chicken to a classic chicken pot pie, chicken has become a must-have kitchen staple with wonderful versatility. You can fry it, barbecue it, roast it, saute it or find it rotisserie or deli-style in your local grocery store. Whether you're counting calories, carbohydrates, fat grams, your hard-earned pennies or your blessings, chicken is a perfect choice 365 days a year because it's a simple, economical choice for healthy, hearty meals.

The National Chicken Council estimates that American consumers put about 26 billion pounds of chicken in their grocery carts in 2005. That's an amazing 87 pounds of bird for every man, woman and child in the U.S. People simply love chicken!

We bring you the ultimate chicken cookbook to give you a bird's eye view of the variety of ways to bring chicken to the table with numerous time-saving dishes perfect for a quick dinner for the family after a hectic day or a dinner party for family and friends. This book strives to give you more of what you want – tasty and delectable chicken recipes that will save you time, effort and make your life simpler and more enjoyable.

From skillets to wraps to exciting grilling ideas, ***365 Easy Chicken Recipes*** proves there's no limit to the delicious ways to cook the bird. Try **Chicken-Tortilla Dumplings**, a fun twist on traditional chicken and dumplings. Or how about serving up a skillet dish with **Crunchy Chip Chicken**? **Dad's Best Smoked Chicken** is also an excellent choice with its excellent 7UP® marinade with a kick. Many of our recipes have that special something like a great technique or a knockout sauce. If you love chicken as we do, you will now have 365 more reasons to crave leftovers.

 # Contents

> *Bone up on your chicken history. Chickens have come a long way since they were depicted in Babylonian carvings in 600 B.C. and were believed to have had special powers.*

> *Quick, beak-watering chicken starters ranging from imaginative finger fare to hearty soups that will have your guests crowing for more.*

> *Please your flock with these simple, innovative chicken casseroles that are anything but ordinary. Each one is unique with its own distinct flavor, colorful combination of vegetables, cheeses and pastas. And all taste great!*

Contents

Chicken: The Early Days

The chicken is believed to have originated at least 4,000 years ago in Asia, a region where some of the world's finest chicken recipes come from. There is evidence that centuries ago, people realized the value of chicken and raised chickens to provide meat and eggs as well. For example, chickens are depicted in Babylonian carvings as far back as 600 B.C. and mentioned by early Greek writers, such as the playwright Aristophanes in 400 B.C. Indeed, the Romans considered chickens valuable and even sacred to Mars, the God of War.

In ancient Rome, people believed chickens had special powers and they used them to predict the future. They also had a great number of recipes that involved chicken and eggs. Romans had several breeds of chickens and ate every part of the chicken, including the livers, gizzards and stomach.

U.S. Chicken Industry History

The chicken industry in the United States is one of the most successful sectors in agriculture. In just 50 years, the U.S. broiler industry has evolved from fragmented, locally oriented businesses into a highly efficient, vertically integrated, progressive success story increasingly supplying customers nationwide and around the globe. The modern chicken industry produces nutritious, wholesome, high-quality products that become more affordable year after year.

During the late 1800s through the early 1900s, early poultry production consisted of many households having backyard flocks of dual-purpose chickens. These chickens supplied eggs and an occasional chicken for Sunday or holiday dinner. By the turn of the century, a few entrepreneurs began selling young chickens during the summer for meat as a sideline activity on their family farms.

By the 1960s, the commercial broiler industry began its economic boom. The specially bred meat chickens (broilers) surpassed farm chickens as the number one source of chicken meat in the United States. In the late 1960s and early 1970s, chicken-producing companies used television and print media to market chickens under brand names.

Chicken consumption surpassed beef consumption in the U.S. in 1992. Chicken had already surpassed pork consumption in 1985.

Dedication

With a mission of helping you bring family and friends to the table, Cookbook Resources strives to make family meals and entertaining friends simple, easy and delicious.

We recognize the importance of a meal together as a means of building family bonds with memories and traditions that will be treasured for a lifetime. It is an opportunity to sit down with each other and share more than food.

This cookbook is dedicated with gratitude and respect for all those who show their love with homecooked meals, bringing family and friends to the table.

*More and more statistical studies are finding that family
meals play a significant role in childhood development.
Children who eat with their families four or more nights
per week are healthier, make better grades, score higher on
aptitude tests and are less likely to have problems with drugs.*

Wings 'n Things

Quick, beak-watering chicken starters ranging from imaginative finger fare to hearty soups that will have your guests crowing for more.

Wings 'n Things Contents

Chili-Honeyed Wings

18 - 20 wing drummettes
and wing portions

1 cup flour	120 g
¼ cup (½ stick) butter	60 ml
⅔ cup honey	230 g
⅔ cup chili sauce	180 g
2 teaspoons minced garlic	10 ml

- Preheat oven to 325° (160° C).

- Press each wing in flour mixed with a little salt and cover well.

- Melt butter in large skillet. Brown chicken wings over medium-high heat and place in sprayed 9 x 13-inch (23 x 33 cm) glass baking dish.

- Combine honey, chili sauce and garlic in small bowl and stir well.

- Spoon honey mixture over each wing and make sure some of sauce covers each wing.

- Cover and bake for 1 hour. Yields 18 to 20 wings.

Flautas de Pollo

Traditional flautas are filled with beef, chicken or pork and work as a main course, appetizer or side dish.

1 cup cooked, minced chicken	140 g
12 flour tortillas	
Canola oil	
Guacamole	
Salsa	

- Spoon 1 rounded tablespoon (15 ml) chicken in center of each tortilla and roll into tight tube. Heat about 1 inch (2.5 cm) oil to about 350° (175° C) in 4-quart (4 L) roasting pan or large, heavy pan.

- Fry flautas in oil, turn once to brown on both sides and drain.

- Serve with choice of guacamole or salsa. Yields 12 flautas.

Deluxe Dinner Nachos

Nachos:

1 (14 ounce) package tortilla
   chips, divided   400 g
1 (8 ounce) package shredded
   Velveeta® cheese,
   divided   230 g
1 (8 ounce) can chopped
   jalapenos, divided   230 g

Deluxe Nacho Topping:

1 (11 ounce) can Mexicorn®
   with liquid   310 g
1 (15 ounce) can jalapeno
   pinto beans   425 g
2 cups skinned, chopped
   rotisserie chicken   280 g
1 bunch fresh green onions,
   chopped
Salsa

- Preheat oven to 400° (205° C).

- Place about three-quarters of tortilla chips in sprayed baking dish. Sprinkle half cheese and about 3 jalapenos on top. Heat just until cheese melts.

- Combine Mexicorn®, beans and rotisserie chicken in saucepan. Heat over medium heat, stirring constantly, until mixture is hot. Spoon mixture over nachos, place dish in oven and heat for about 10 minutes.

- Sprinkle remaining cheese and green onions over top and serve immediately. Garnish with remaining jalapenos, remaining tortilla chips and salsa. Serves 8.

Chimichangas con Pollo

Chimichangas are deep-fried stuffed tortillas. Tucson claims to be the birthplace of the chimichanga or chimi.

4 - 6 boneless, skinless chicken breast halves, cooked, shredded
3 - 4 New Mexico green chiles, roasted, peeled, chopped
2 tomatoes, peeled, seeded, chopped
1 onion, chopped finely
6 - 8 flour tortillas
1 (8 ounce) package shredded Mexican 4-cheese blend   230 g
Red or green chile sauce

- Combine chicken, green chiles, tomatoes and onion and stir well to mix. Divide mixture evenly onto tortillas and top with cheese. Fold ends like envelope, roll and secure with toothpick.

- Place in deep fryer with oil heated to 350° (175° C) and fry until golden brown. Drain and serve with chile sauce. Serves 4.

When choosing a package of fresh chicken breasts, look for one that isn't too "juicy." Water is a sure sign of thawing. Look for medium-size, uniform breasts that will cook in the same amount of time.

Turkey Jerky

One of the best things in South Texas is turkey jerky and it is found in many local grocery stores.

Turkey breasts, cooked

- Preheat oven to 175° (80° C).

- Slice turkey breasts across the grain in very thin slices about ¼-inch (6 mm) thick.

- Place on baking sheet and sprinkle both sides lightly with salt and a lot of freshly ground black pepper.

- Cook in oven until turkey gets to the right consistency. It should be very dense, dark brown, but not burned. (The time is different with the size of pieces. Beef jerky takes 6 to 8 hours or more, but turkey jerky usually takes less time. Adjust time according to taste.) Serves 3 to 4.

Easy Crispy Chicken Tacos

Everybody goes for this classic. Crispy taco shells with chicken, beef or fish make great Southwest treats.

8 - 10 taco shells, warmed	
4 - 6 boneless, skinless chicken breast halves, cooked, chopped	
1 cup diced tomato, drained	255 g
½ cup diced onion	110 g
1 cup chopped lettuce	80 g
1 (12 ounce) package shredded cheddar cheese	340 g
1 (8 ounce) jar spicy salsa	230 g

- Make tacos by filling each taco shell with chicken, tomato, onion, lettuce and cheese. Serve with salsa. Serves 4 to 6.

Chicken for Lunch

4 cooked, thick chicken
   breast slices from deli
1 (3 ounce) package cream
   cheese, softened   85 g
3 tablespoons salsa   40 g
2 tablespoons mayonnaise   30 g

- Place chicken slices on serving platter.

- Beat cream cheese, salsa and mayonnaise in bowl until smooth and creamy.

- Place 1 heaping tablespoon (15 ml) cream cheese mixture on top of each chicken slice and serve cold. Serves 4.

Cracked-Pepper Turkey Breast

This is a delicious turkey breast that can be served many ways. Leftovers are great in turkey sandwiches and turkey casserole.

1 (2½ - 3 pound) refrigerated
   cooked, cracked
   pepper turkey
   breast   1.1 - 1.4 kg
1 (16 ounce) jar hot
   chipotle salsa   455 g
1 (8 ounce) package
   shredded 4-cheese
   blend   230 g

- Slice enough turkey for each person. Spoon 1 heaping tablespoon (15 ml) chipotle salsa over each slice and sprinkle a little cheese over top. Serves 6.

Turkey Tenders with Honey-Ginger Glaze

Canola oil
1 pound turkey tenders   **455 g**
Rice, cooked

- Place a little oil in heavy skillet and cook turkey tenders for about 5 minutes on each side or until they brown.

Avoid cross-contamination of utensils used on raw poultry and avoid packages that leak.

Glaze:

⅔ **cup honey**	**230 g**
2 teaspoons peeled grated	
fresh ginger	**10 ml**
1 tablespoon white wine	
Worcestershire sauce	**15 ml**
1 tablespoon soy sauce	**15 ml**
1 tablespoon lemon juice	**15 ml**

- Combine all glaze ingredients in bowl, mix well and pour into skillet. Bring mixture to a boil, reduce heat and simmer for 15 minutes. Serve over rice. Serves 4.

TIP: *You might want to try the new packages of rice that can be microwaved for 90 seconds – and it's ready to serve.*

Chicken-Noodle Soup Supper

1 (3 ounce) package
   chicken-flavored
   ramen noodles, broken   85 g
1 (10 ounce) package frozen
   green peas, thawed   280 g
1 (4 ounce) jar sliced
   mushrooms, drained   115 g
3 cups cooked, cubed chicken   420 g

- Heat 2¼ cups (560 g) water in large saucepan to boiling. Add ramen noodles, contents of seasoning packet and peas. Heat to boiling, reduce heat to medium and cook for about 5 minutes.

- Stir in mushrooms and chicken and continue cooking over low heat until all ingredients are hot. To serve, spoon into soup bowls. Serves 6.

Five-Can Soup Bowl

1 (14 ounce) can
   chicken broth   400 g
1 (10 ounce) can cream of
   chicken soup   280 g
1 (12 ounce) can
   chicken breast   340 g
1 (15 ounce) can
   ranch-style beans   425 g
1 (10 ounce) can tomatoes
   and green chilies   280 g
Tortilla chips, crushed
   coarsely
Shredded cheese
Sour cream

- Combine broth, soup, chicken, beans and tomatoes and green chilies in saucepan and simmer for 30 minutes. Serve over tortilla chips and top with cheese and sour cream. Serves 6.

Northern Chili

2 onions, coarsely chopped
Olive oil
3 (15 ounce) cans great
    northern beans, drained
    3 (425 g)
2 (14 ounce) cans
    chicken broth   2 (400 g)
2 tablespoons
    minced garlic   30 ml
1 (7 ounce) can chopped
    green chilies   200 g
1 tablespoon
    ground cumin   15 ml
3 cups cooked, finely
    chopped chicken
    breasts   420 g
1 (8 ounce) package
    shredded Monterey
    Jack cheese   230 g

- Cook onions with a little oil in large, heavy pot for about 5 minutes, but do not brown.

- Place 1 can beans in shallow bowl and mash with fork. Combine mashed beans, 2 remaining cans of beans, chicken broth, garlic, green chilies and cumin in saucepan. Bring to a boil and reduce heat.

- Cover and simmer for 30 minutes. Add chopped chicken, stir to blend well and heat until chili is thoroughly hot. When serving, top each bowl with 3 tablespoons (20 g) cheese. Serves 6.

Q: What do you get if you cross a chicken with a cement mixer?

A: A bricklayer.

Chicken-Vegetable Stew Pot

1 (16 ounce) package frozen, chopped onions and bell peppers	455 g
Olive oil	
2 tablespoons minced garlic	30 ml
2 tablespoons chili powder	30 ml
3 teaspoons ground cumin	15 ml
2 pounds cooked chicken tenderloin, cubed	910 g
2 (14 ounce) cans chicken broth	2 (400 g)
3 (15 ounce) cans pinto beans with jalapenos, divided	3 (425 g)

- Cook onions and bell peppers with a little oil in skillet for about 5 minutes, stirring occasionally. Add garlic, chili powder, cumin and cubed chicken and cook an additional 5 minutes.

- Stir in broth and a little salt. Bring to a boil and reduce heat. Cover and simmer for 15 minutes.

- Place 1 can beans in shallow bowl and mash with fork. Add mashed beans and remaining 2 cans beans to pot. Bring to boil, reduce heat and simmer for 10 minutes. Serves 8.

Hearty 15-Minute Turkey Soup

1 (14 ounce) can chicken broth	400 g
3 (15 ounce) cans navy beans, rinsed, drained	3 (425 g)
1 (28 ounce) can diced tomatoes with liquid	795 g
2 - 3 cups small chunks cooked white turkey meat	280 - 420 g
2 teaspoons minced garlic	10 ml
¼ teaspoon cayenne pepper	1 ml
Freshly grated parmesan cheese for garnish	

- Mix all ingredients except cheese in saucepan and heat. Garnish with parmesan cheese before serving. Serves 6.

Day-After-Thanksgiving Turkey Chili

3 pounds ground turkey	1.4 kg
½ teaspoon garlic powder	2 ml
3 tablespoons chili powder	45 ml
1 (8 ounce) can tomato sauce	230 g
Shredded cheese	

- Combine turkey and garlic powder with 1 cup (250 ml) water in large saucepan. Cook over medium heat until mixture begins to fry.

- Add chili powder and tomato sauce and simmer until meat is tender. Garnish with cheese. Serves 6.

Old-Fashioned Chicken and Dumplings

2 pounds boneless, skinless	
chicken breasts	**910 g**
½ onion, chopped	
½ cup sliced celery	**50 g**
1 carrot, sliced	
3 tablespoons shortening	**30 g**
2 cups flour	**240 g**

- Place chicken breasts and cover with water in large soup pot.

- Add onion, celery, carrot, 1 teaspoon (5 ml) salt and ½ teaspoon (2 ml) pepper.

- Cover and cook for 40 minutes or until chicken is tender. Remove chicken and break into bite-size pieces

- Strain broth and return to pot.

- Cut shortening into flour and 1 teaspoon (5 ml) salt in large bowl with pastry blender or fork until dough is pea-size. Add 9 tablespoons (135 ml) ice water one at a time and mix lightly with fork.

- On floured surface, roll dough very thinly and keep rolling pin well floured. Cut into strips and layer on wax paper. Refrigerate for 45 minutes.

- Bring broth and chicken pieces to boil. Drop strips into boiling broth and chicken pieces. Do not stir, just jiggle or shake pot. (Stirring will break up dumplings.) Cook on medium heat for 30 minutes. Serves 8.

Hot Gobble Gobble Soup

This is spicy, but not too much, just right!

3 - 4 cups cooked chopped turkey	**420 - 560 g**
3 (10 ounce) cans condensed chicken broth	**3 (280 g)**
2 (10 ounce) cans diced tomatoes and green chilies	**2 (280 g)**
1 (15 ounce) can whole corn, drained	**425 g**
1 large onion, chopped	
1 (10 ounce) can tomato soup	**280 g**
1 teaspoon garlic powder	**5 ml**
1 teaspoon dried oregano	**5 ml**
3 tablespoons cornstarch	**25 g**

- Combine turkey, broth, tomatoes and green chilies, corn, onion, tomato soup, garlic powder and oregano in large roasting pan.

- Mix cornstarch with 3 tablespoons (45 ml) water and add to soup mixture. Bring to a boil, reduce heat and simmer, stirring occasionally for about 2 hours. Serves 6.

Never partially cook poultry and store to finish later. The heat may simply start cultivating bacteria that will be thriving too strongly to be fully destroyed by the briefer cooking time when you finish cooking it.

White Lightning Chili

1½ cups dried navy beans	395 g
3 (14 ounce) cans chicken broth	3 (400 g)
2 tablespoons butter	30 g
1 onion, chopped	
1 clove garlic, minced	
3 cups chopped, cooked chicken	420 g
1 (4 ounce) can chopped green chilies	115 g
½ teaspoon dried basil	2 ml
1½ teaspoons ground cumin	7 ml
½ teaspoon dried oregano	2 ml
6 (8 inch) flour tortillas	6 (20 cm)
Shredded Monterey Jack cheese	

- Wash beans and place in large, heavy pan. Cover with water 2 inches (5 cm) above beans and soak overnight. Drain beans, add broth, butter, 1 cup (250 ml) water, onion and garlic and bring to boil. Reduce heat, cover and simmer for 2 hours 30 minutes. Stir occasionally.

- With potato masher, mash half of beans. Add chicken, green chilies, basil, ½ teaspoon (2 ml) pepper, cumin and oregano. Bring to a boil, reduce heat, cover and simmer for an additional 30 minutes.

- With kitchen shears, make 4 cuts in each tortilla toward center, but not through center. Line serving bowls with tortillas and overlap cut edges. Spoon in chili and top with cheese. Serves 6.

TIP: *Some people like to add ⅛ teaspoon (.5 ml) each of cayenne pepper and ground cloves.*

Chicken Waldorf Salad

1 pound boneless, skinless chicken breasts	455 g
1 red with peel, sliced	
1 green apple with peel, sliced	
1 cup sliced celery	100 g
½ cup chopped walnuts	65 g
2 (6 ounce) cartons orange yogurt	2 (170 g)
½ cup mayonnaise	110 g
1 (6 ounce) package shredded lettuce	170 g

- Place chicken in large saucepan and cover with water. Cook on high heat for about 15 minutes, drain and cool. Cut into 1-inch (2.5 cm) chucks, season with salt and pepper and place in large salad bowl.

- Add sliced apples, celery and walnuts. Stir in yogurt and mayonnaise and toss to mix well. (May be served room temperature or refrigerate for several hours.) Serve over shredded lettuce. Serves 6.

A comb is the flesh on the top of a chicken's head.

Chicken Medley Supreme

1 cup chopped onion	160 g
1 cup chopped celery	100 g
Olive oil	
1 (6 ounce) package long grain-wild rice, cooked	170 g
1 (10 ounce) can cream of chicken soup	280 g
1 (4 ounce) jar chopped pimentos	115 g
1 (15 ounce) can French-style green beans, drained	425 g
½ cup slivered almonds	85 g
1 cup mayonnaise	225 g
3 cups lightly crushed potato chips	170 g

- Preheat oven to 350° (175° C).

- Saute onion and celery with a little oil in skillet. Combine all ingredients in large bowl except potato chips. Season with a little salt and pepper.

- Spray 9 x 13-inch (23 x 33 cm) baking dish and spoon mixture into dish. Sprinkle crushed potato chips over casserole and bake for 35 minute or until chips are light brown. Serves 8.

After-Thanksgiving Salad

2 (10 ounce) packages	
romaine lettuce	2 (280 g)
2½ - 3 cups cooked,	
sliced turkey	350 - 420 g
1 (8 ounce) jar baby	
corn, quartered	230 g
2 tomatoes, chopped	
1 (8 ounce) package	
shredded colby	
cheese	230 g

• Combine romaine lettuce, turkey, baby corn, tomatoes and cheese in large salad bowl.

Dressing:

⅔ cup mayonnaise	150 g
⅔ cup salsa	175 g
¼ cup cider vinegar	60 ml
2 tablespoons sugar	25 g

• Combine all dressing ingredients in bowl. When ready to serve sprinkle with a little salt and pepper, spoon dressing over salad and toss to coat well. Serves 4.

TIP: *This is a wonderful salad just like this, but if you have some ripe olives, red onion, black beans or precooked bacon, throw it in the bowl. It will be even better.*

Pasta-Turkey Salad Supper

1 (12 ounce) package tri-color spiral pasta	340 g
1 (4 ounce) can sliced ripe olives, drained	115 g
1 cup each fresh broccoli and cauliflower florets	71 g/100 g
2 small yellow squash, sliced	
1 cup halved cherry tomatoes	150 g
1 (8 ounce) bottle cheddar-parmesan ranch dressing	230 g
1½ pounds hickory-smoked cracked-pepper turkey breast, sliced	680 g

- Cook pasta according to package directions. Drain and rinse in cold water. Combine add olives, broccoli, cauliflower, sliced squash and tomatoes in large salad bowl.

- Toss with dressing. Place thin slices of turkey breast, arranged in rows, over salad. Serve immediately. Serves 8.

Chickens and turkeys are known to cross-breed and are known as "turkins."

Cheesy Caesar Pizza

1(12 inch) Italian pizza crust	32 cm
1 (8 ounce) package shredded mozzarella cheese	230 g
1 (6 ounce) package cooked chicken breast strips	170 g
2 cups shredded lettuce	155 g
3 fresh green onions, sliced	
¾ cup shredded cheddar-colby cheese	85 g
½ (8 ounce) bottle Caesar dressing	½ (230 g)

- Preheat oven to 400° (205° C).

- Top pizza crust with mozzarella cheese and bake for 8 minutes or until cheese melts.

- Combine chicken strips, lettuce, onions and cheese in bowl. Pour about half of Caesar dressing over salad and toss.

- Top hot pizza with salad and cut into wedges. Serve immediately. Serves 4.

Q: Why did the chicken cross the road?

A: To prove to the armadillo that it could be done.

Raisin-Rice Chicken Salad

3 cups instant brown rice	285 g
¼ cup (½ stick) butter	60 g
3 cups finely chopped cooked chicken breasts	420 g
½ cup golden raisins	75 g
½ cup chopped red bell pepper	75 g

- Cook brown rice according to package directions. Add butter and a little salt and pepper. While rice is still hot, stir in cubed chicken, raisins and bell pepper. Transfer to serving bowl.

Dressing:

2 tablespoons lemon juice	30 ml
1 tablespoon dijon-style mustard	15 ml
2 tablespoons honey	45 g
1 teaspoon white wine vinegar	5 ml
¼ cup slivered almonds, toasted	40 g

- Combine lemon juice, mustard, honey and wine vinegar in jar and shake until ingredients blend well. Drizzle over rice-chicken mixture and sprinkle with almonds. Serves 4.

TIP: *Toasting brings out the flavors of nuts and seeds. Place nuts or seeds on baking sheet and bake at 225° (110° C) for 10 minutes. Be careful not to burn them.*

Bridge Club Luncheon Chicken

1 rotisserie-cooked chicken
1 cup red or green grapes,
    halved   150 g
2 cups chopped celery   200 g
⅔ cup whole walnuts   90 g
⅔ cup sliced fresh onion   110 g

- Skin chicken, cut chicken breast in thin strips and place in bowl with lid. (Reserve dark meat for another use.) Add red or green grapes, celery, walnuts and sliced onions.

Dressing:

½ cup mayonnaise   110 g
1 tablespoon orange juice   15 ml
2 tablespoons red wine
    vinegar   30 ml
1 teaspoon chili powder   5 ml
1 teaspoon paprika   5 ml

- Combine all dressing ingredients in bowl, add a little salt and pepper and mix well. Spoon over salad mixture and toss. Serves 8.

Q: What do you get when you cross a chicken and a pit bull?

A: Just the pit bull.

Luscious Papaya-Chicken Salad

1 (10 ounce) package
   romaine lettuce, torn   **280 g**
2 ripe papayas, peeled,
   seeded, cubed
1 large red bell pepper,
   seeded, sliced
2 cups cooked, cubed
   chicken breasts   **280 g**
⅓ cup pecan pieces, toasted   **40 g**

- Combine lettuce, papayas and bell pepper in large salad bowl. Whisk lime juice, honey, garlic, mustard and a little salt in small bowl. Slowly add olive oil in thin stream and whisk dressing until it blends well.

Dressing:

¼ cup lime juice   **60 ml**
¼ cup honey   **35 g**
2 teaspoons minced garlic   **10 ml**
1 teaspoon dijon-style
   mustard   **5 ml**
3 tablespoons extra-virgin
   olive oil   **45 ml**

- Combine dressing ingredients in bowl and pour over salad, add cubed chicken and toss. To serve, sprinkle pecans over top of salad. Serves 6.

Chicken-Rice Salad Supreme

**2 (5 ounce) cans premium
chunk chicken
breast**   **2 (145 g)**
**2 (9 ounce) packages
whole grain brown
ready-rice**   **2 (255 g)**
**⅔ cup sun-dried
tomatoes**   **35 g**
**2 ripe avocados, peeled,
diced**
**¾ cup dijon-style
mustard vinaigrette
dressing**   **190 g**

- Drain chicken, separate into chunks and save broth. Prepare 2 microwave rice pouches (ready in 90 seconds) according to package directions.

- Combine chicken, rice, tomatoes and avocado in bowl.

- In separate bowl, combine vinaigrette dressing and ½ teaspoon (2 ml) salt. Gently stir into chicken-rice mixture and refrigerate for 2 hours before serving. Serves 8.

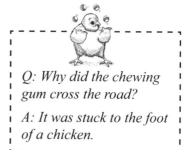

Q: Why did the chewing gum cross the road?

A: It was stuck to the foot of a chicken.

Chinese Chicken Salad

2 cups cooked, chopped chicken	280 g
1 cup diced celery	100 g
1 (11 ounce) can mandarin oranges, drained	310 g
⅓ cup sliced almonds, toasted	65 g
¾ cup whipped topping	55 g
¾ cup Catalina dressing	175 ml
1 cup chow mein noodles	55 g

• Mix chicken, celery, mandarin oranges and almonds in large bowl.

• In separate bowl, mix whipped topping, dressing, noodles and ½ teaspoon (2 ml) salt.

• Combine dressing with salad and serve immediately. Serves 6.

TIP: You can make the salad in advance, but mix the dressing right before serving.

Barbecue-Chicken Salad

Dressing:

¾ cup ranch dressing	175 ml
3 tablespoons barbecue sauce	45 g
2 tablespoons salsa	35 g

• Combine all dressing ingredients in bowl and refrigerate.

Salad:

3 boneless, skinless chicken breasts, grilled	
1 (9 ounce) package romaine lettuce, torn	255 g
1 (15 ounce) can seasoned black beans, rinsed, drained	425 g
12 - 15 cherry tomatoes	

• Cut chicken breasts in strips and heat. Place chicken strips, romaine, black beans and cherry tomatoes in bowl and toss with enough dressing to lightly coat. Serves 6 to 8.

Strawberry-Chicken Salad

1 pound boneless, skinless chicken breast halves	455 g
Olive oil	
1 (10 ounce) package spring greens mix	280 g
1 pint fresh strawberries, sliced	455 g
½ cup chopped walnuts	65 g

Dressing:

¾ cup honey	255 g
⅔ cup red wine vinegar	150 ml
1 tablespoon soy sauce	15 ml
½ teaspoon ground ginger	2 ml

- Cut chicken into strips and place in large skillet with a little oil. Cook and stir on medium-high heat for about 10 minutes.

- While chicken cooks, combine all dressing ingredients in bowl and mix well. After chicken strips cook, pour ½ cup (125 ml) dressing into skillet with chicken and cook additional 2 minutes or until liquid evaporates.

- Combine spring greens mix, strawberries and walnuts in salad bowl. Pour in remaining dressing and toss. Top with chicken strips. Serves 6.

Q: Why was the chicken afraid of the chicken?

A: Because he was chicken.

Beak-Pleasing Casseroles

Please your flock with these simple, innovative chicken casseroles that are anything but ordinary. Each one is unique with its own distinct flavor, colorful combination of vegetables, cheeses and pastas. And all taste great!

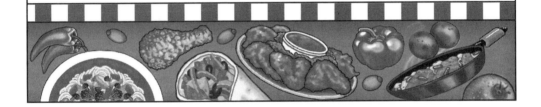

Beak-Pleasing Casseroles Contents

Beak-Pleasing Casseroles Contents

3-Cheese Turkey Casserole

1 (8 ounce) package egg noodles	230 g
1 teaspoon olive oil	5 ml
3 tablespoons butter	35 g
¾ cup chopped green bell pepper	110 g
½ cup chopped celery	50 g
½ cup chopped onion	80 g
1 (10 ounce) can cream of chicken soup	280 g
½ cup milk	125 ml
1 (6 ounce) jar whole mushrooms	170 g
1 (16 ounce) carton small curd cottage cheese	455 g
4 cups diced cooked turkey or chicken	1 L
1 (12 ounce) package shredded cheddar cheese	340 g
¾ cup freshly grated parmesan cheese	75 g

- Preheat oven to 350° (175° C).

- Place noodles in 3 quarts (3 L) hot water, add 1 tablespoon (15 ml) salt and oil in large soup pot and cook according to package directions.

- Melt butter in skillet and saute bell pepper, celery and onion.

- Combine noodles, bell pepper-onion mixture, chicken soup, milk, mushrooms, ½ teaspoon (2 ml) pepper, cottage cheese, turkey and cheddar cheese in large bowl.

- Pour into sprayed 9 x 13-inch (23 x 33 cm) baking dish and top with parmesan cheese. Bake for 40 minutes. Serves 10.

Chucky Clucky Casserole

1 (16 ounce) package frozen broccoli spears	455 g
3 cups cooked, diced chicken	420 g
1 (10 ounce) can cream of chicken soup	280 g
2 tablespoons milk	30 ml
⅓ cup mayonnaise	75 g
2 teaspoons lemon juice	10 ml
3 tablespoons butter, melted	35 g
1 cup breadcrumbs or cracker crumbs	60 g
⅓ cup shredded cheddar cheese	40 g

- Preheat oven to 350° (175° C).

- Cook broccoli according to package directions and drain.

- Place broccoli in sprayed 9 x 13-inch (23 x 33 cm) glass baking dish. Sprinkle 1 teaspoon (5 ml) salt over broccoli and cover with diced chicken.

- Combine soup, milk, mayonnaise, lemon juice and ¼ teaspoon (1 ml) pepper in saucepan. Heat just enough to dilute soup a little and pour over chicken.

- Mix melted butter, breadcrumbs and cheese in bowl and sprinkle over soup mixture. Bake for 30 minutes or until mixture is hot and bubbly. Serves 8.

Easy Chicken Enchiladas

10 corn tortillas
1 (10 ounce) can golden
   mushroom soup   280 g
1 (10 ounce) can cream
   of chicken soup   280 g
1 cup milk   250 ml
1 small onion, chopped
2 (7 ounce) cans green
   chile salsa   2 (200 g)
4 - 5 boneless, skinless
   chicken breast halves,
   cooked
1 (12 ounce) package
   shredded cheddar
   cheese   340 g

- Preheat oven to 350° (175° C).

- Cut tortillas into 1-inch (2.5 cm) strips and lay half of them in sprayed, 9 x 13-inch (23 x 33 cm) baking dish.

- Mix mushroom soup, chicken soup, milk, onion and salsa in saucepan and heat just enough to mix.

- Chop cooked chicken and place half on top of tortilla strips in baking dish. Pour half of sauce on top of chicken, repeat tortilla layer and sauce layer.

- Cover and bake for 45 minutes. Uncover, sprinkle with cheese and bake for an additional 10 minutes. Serve hot. Serves 8.

Q: How do chickens bake a cake?

A: From scratch.

Busy Day Chicken Casserole

6 boneless, skinless
   chicken breast
   halves, cooked
1 (1 pint) carton
   sour cream   455 g
1 (7 ounce) package
   ready-cut spaghetti   200 g
2 (10 ounce) cans cream
   of chicken soup   2 (280 g)
1 (4 ounce) can
   mushrooms, drained   115 g
½ cup (1 stick) butter,
   melted   115 g
1 cup fresh grated
   parmesan cheese   100 g

- Preheat oven to 350° (175° C).

- Cut chicken into strips and combine all ingredients, except parmesan cheese with ⅛ teaspoon (.5 ml) pepper in bowl and mix well.

- Pour into sprayed 9 x 13-inch (23 x 33 cm) baking dish and sprinkle cheese on top. Bake covered for 50 minutes. Serves 6.

Hot-n-Sour Chicky Casserole

1 (3 ounce) package
   chicken-flavored instant
   ramen noodles   85 g
1 (16 ounce) package frozen
   broccoli, cauliflower
   and carrots   455 g
⅔ cup sweet-and-sour sauce   180 g
3 boneless, skinless chicken
   breast halves, cooked

- Cook noodles and vegetables and 2 cups (500 ml) boiling water in saucepan for 3 minutes, stir occasionally and drain.

- Add contents of seasoning packet, sweet-and-sour sauce and a little salt and pepper to noodle mixture.

- Cut chicken in strips, add chicken to noodle mixture and heat thoroughly. Serves 6.

Turkey-Broccoli Bake

**1 (16 ounce) package frozen
broccoli spears, thawed   455 g
2 cups cooked, diced leftover
turkey or chicken   280 g**

- Preheat oven to 350° (175° C).

- Arrange broccoli spears
  in sprayed 9 x 13-inch
  (23 x 33 cm) baking dish and
  sprinkle with diced turkey.

Sauce:

**1 (10 ounce) can cream of
chicken soup   280 g
½ cup mayonnaise   110 g
2 tablespoons lemon juice   30 ml
⅓ cup grated parmesan
cheese   35 g**

- Combine chicken soup,
  mayonnaise, lemon juice, cheese
  and ¼ cup (60 ml) water in
  saucepan. Heat just enough to
  mix well.

- Spoon over broccoli and turkey.
  Cover and bake for 20 minutes,
  uncover and continue baking
  for an additional 15 minutes.
  Serves 6 to 8.

*The term "cull" refers
to removing a bird from
the flock because
of productivity,
age, health or
personality issues.*

Chicken-Tortilla Dumplings

This is a great recipe and using tortillas is a lot easier than making real dumplings!

6 large boneless, skinless
  chicken breast halves,
  cubed
2 ribs celery, chopped
1 onion, chopped
2 tablespoons chicken
  bouillon granules   30 ml
1 (10 ounce) can cream
  of chicken soup   280 g
10 (8 inch) flour tortillas   10 (20 cm)

- Place chicken breasts, 10 cups (2 L) water, celery and onion in roasting pan.

- Bring to a boil, reduce heat and cook about 30 minutes or until chicken is tender. Remove chicken and set aside to cool.

- Save broth in roasting pan (about 9 cups/2 L broth). Add chicken bouillon and taste to make sure it is rich and tasty. (Add more bouillon if needed and more water if you don't have 9 cups/2 L broth.) Add chicken soup to broth and bring to boil.

- Cut tortillas into 2 x 1-inch (5 x 2.5 cm) strips. Add strips, one at a time, to briskly boiling broth mixture and stir constantly.

- When all strips are in saucepan, pour in chicken, reduce heat to low and simmer for 5 to 10 minutes. Stir well but gently to prevent dumplings from sticking. (The pot of chicken and dumplings will be very thick.)

- Pour into very large serving bowl and serve hot. Serves 10.

Rule-the-Roost Casserole

1 (7 ounce) box chicken-flavored rice and macaroni	200 g
1 (10 ounce) can cream of mushroom soup	280 g
1 (10 ounce) can cream of celery soup	280 g
3 cups cooked, chopped chicken or turkey	420 g
1 (10 ounce) package frozen peas, thawed	280 g
1 cup shredded cheddar cheese	115 g

- Preheat oven to 350° (175° C).

- Cook rice and macaroni according to package directions. Mix both soups with ½ cup (125 ml) water.

- Combine chicken, cooked rice and macaroni, soups, peas and cheese in bowl and mix well.

- Pour into sprayed 3-quart (3 L) baking dish and bake covered for 40 minutes. Serves 6.

Cheesy Chick Bake

8 boneless, skinless chicken breast halves	
8 slices Swiss cheese	
1 (10 ounce) can cream of chicken soup	280 g
1 (8 ounce) box chicken stuffing mix	230 g

- Preheat oven to 325° (160° C).

- Flatten each chicken breast with rolling pin and place in sprayed 9 x 13-inch (23 x 33 cm) baking dish.

- Place cheese slices over chicken.

- Combine chicken soup and ½ cup (125 ml) water and pour over chicken.

- Prepare stuffing mix according to package directions and sprinkle over chicken.

- Bake for 1 hour. Serves 8.

Chicken Breasts Supreme

**6 boneless, skinless chicken
    breast halves**

¼ cup (½ stick) butter	**60 ml**
**1 (10 ounce) can cream of
chicken soup**	**280 g**
**¾ cup sauterne or chicken
broth**	**175 ml**
**1 (8.5 ounce) can sliced water
chestnuts, drained**	**240 g**
**1 (4 ounce) can sliced
mushrooms, drained**	**115 g**
**2 tablespoons chopped green
bell peppers**	**20 g**
**¼ teaspoon crushed thyme
leaves**	**1 ml**

- Preheat oven to 350° (175° C).

- Brown chicken breasts in butter on all sides in skillet. Arrange in 9 x 13-inch (23 x 33 cm) baking pan. Sprinkle with ½ teaspoon (2 ml) salt and dash of pepper.

- Add soup to butter that is left in skillet and slowly stir in sauterne or broth. Add remaining ingredients and heat to boil.

- Pour soup mixture over chicken. Cover and bake for 45 minutes. Remove cover and bake for an additional 15 minutes. Serves 6.

If a rooster is not present in a flock of hens, a hen will often take the role, stop laying and begin to crow.

Chicken Chow Mein

3½ cups cooked, cubed chicken breasts	490 g
2 (10 ounce) cans cream of chicken soup	2 (280 g)
2 (15 ounce) cans chop suey vegetables, drained	2 (425 g)
1 (8 ounce) can sliced water chestnuts, drained	230 g
¾ cup chopped cashew nuts	105 g
1 green bell pepper, seeded, chopped	
1 onion, chopped	
1 cup chopped celery	100 g
¼ teaspoon hot sauce	1 ml
1¼ cups chow mein noodles	70 g

- Preheat oven to 350° (175° C).

- Combine chicken, soup, vegetables, water chestnuts, cashew nuts, bell pepper, onion, celery and hot sauce in large bowl. Stir to mix well.

- Spoon into sprayed 9 x 13-inch (23 x 33 cm) baking dish. Sprinkle chow mein noodles over top of casserole.

- Bake for 35 minutes or until it bubbles at edges of casserole. Let stand for 5 minutes before serving. Serves 8.

Chicken Dish, WOW!

1 (10 ounce) can cream of chicken soup	280 g
1 (10 ounce) can fiesta nacho cheese soup	280 g
1 (5 ounce) can evaporated milk	145 g
2 (15 ounce) cans French-style green beans, drained	2 (425 g)
1 teaspoon chicken bouillon granules	5 ml
4 cups cooked, cubed chicken breasts	560 g
1 red bell pepper, chopped	
2 ribs celery, sliced	
¼ cup chopped onion	40 g
1 cup chow mein noodles	55 g
½ cup slivered almonds	85 g
1 (3 ounce) can fried onion rings	85 g

- Preheat oven to 350° (175° C).

- Combine soup, fiesta nacho cheese soup and evaporated milk in bowl and mix well.

- Fold in green beans, chicken bouillon, chicken, bell pepper, celery, onion, noodles, almonds, and ½ teaspoon (2 ml) each of salt and pepper.

- Spoon into sprayed 9 x 13-inch (23 x 33 cm) baking dish.

- Bake covered for 35 minutes. Remove from oven and sprinkle onion rings over casserole.

- Place back in oven and bake for an additional 10 minutes. Serves 12.

TIP: *This casserole may easily be made ahead of time and baked the next day. Just wait to add the onion rings until you put it in the oven.*

Chicken Divan

2 (10 ounce) packages frozen broccoli	2 (280 g)
4 - 6 boneless, skinless chicken breast halves, cooked, sliced	
2 (10 ounce) cans cream of chicken soup	2 (280 g)
1 cup mayonnaise	225 g
1 teaspoon lemon juice	5 ml
½ teaspoon curry powder or Worcestershire sauce	2 ml
1½ cups shredded sharp cheese, divided	170 g
½ cup seasoned breadcrumbs	60 g
1 teaspoon butter, melted	5 ml

- Preheat oven to 350° (175° C).

- Cook broccoli in saucepan until tender and drain. Arrange broccoli in sprayed 9 x 13-inch (23 x 33 cm) baking dish. Place chicken slices on top.

- Combine soup, mayonnaise, lemon juice, curry and ¾ cup (85 g) cheese in bowl and spread over chicken.

- In separate bowl, combine breadcrumbs and butter and layer over chicken. Sprinkle remaining cheese over top and bake for 25 to 30 minutes. Serves 8.

A boneless chicken breast will cook in less than 10 minutes in a steamer. After you remove the chicken, let it sit uncut for 2 to 3 minutes, and any slight pinkness on the interior will gently finish cooking in the chicken's own steam.

Chicken Spaghetti

3 boneless, skinless chicken
    breasts, boiled
1 (10 ounce) can tomatoes
    and green chilies   280 g
1 (10 ounce) can cream of
    mushroom soup   280 g
1 (8 ounce) package
    shredded cheddar
    cheese   230 g
1 (8 ounce) package
    shredded Velveeta®
    cheese   230 g
1 (12 ounce) package
    spaghetti   340 g

• Preheat oven to 350° (175° C).

• Shred cooked chicken into large
  bowl. Add tomatoes and green
  chilies, soup, cheddar cheese
  and Velveeta® cheese. Boil
  spaghetti according to package
  directions and drain.

• Add to chicken mixture and mix
  well. Pour into 3-quart (3 L)
  baking dish. Cover and bake for
  35 minutes. Serves 8.

Curried Chicken Casserole

1 (10 ounce) box
    chicken-flavored   280 g
1 teaspoon curry powder   5 ml
1 (12 ounce) cans chunk
    white chicken with juice   340 g
⅓ cup raisins, optional   50 g

• Preheat oven to 350° (175° C).

• Prepare rice according to
  package directions.

• Add curry powder and chicken
  with juice and raisins and
  mix well.

• Pour into sprayed 7 x 11-inch
  (18 x 28 cm) baking pan. Cover
  and bake for 15 minutes.
  Serves 6.

Manuel's Fiesta Chicken

½ cup (1 stick) butter	115 g
5 - 6 boneless, skinless chicken breast halves	
2 cups finely crushed cheese crackers	120 g
2 tablespoons taco seasoning mix	30 ml
1 bunch green onions with tops, chopped	
1 teaspoon chicken bouillon	5 ml
1 (1 pint) carton whipping cream	500 ml
1 (8 ounce) package shredded Monterey Jack cheese	230 g
1 (4 ounce) can chopped green chilies, drained	115 g

- Preheat oven to 350° (175° C).

- Melt butter in 9 x 13-inch (23 x 33 cm) baking dish and set aside.

- Pound chicken breasts to ¼-inch (6 mm) thick. Combine cracker crumbs and taco seasoning in bowl and mix well. Dredge chicken in mixture and make sure crumbs stick to chicken.

- Place chicken breasts in baking dish with butter. Remove several tablespoons melted butter from dish and place in saucepan. Add onions and saute. Reduce heat and add chicken bouillon.

- Stir well and add whipping cream, cheese and green chilies. Pour mixture over chicken in baking dish and bake for 55 minutes. Serves 8.

Chicken Martinez

1 (10 ounce) can fiesta nacho
   cheese soup   280 g
1 (10 ounce) can cream of
   chicken soup   280 g
1 (8 ounce) carton sour
   cream   230 g
1 onion, chopped
1 (10 ounce) can diced
   tomatoes and green
   chilies   280 g
1 (15 ounce) can black
   beans, rinsed,
   drained   425 g
1 (15 ounce) can whole kernel
   Mexicorn®, drained   425 g
1 teaspoon chili powder   5 ml
8 flour tortillas, cut into
   strips
4 - 5 large boneless, skinless
   chicken breast halves,
   cooked, cut into strips
1 (8 ounce) package shredded
   Mexican 4-cheese blend   230 g

- Preheat oven to 350° (175° C).

- Combine soups, sour cream, onion, tomatoes and green chilies, black beans, corn and chili powder in large bowl and mix well.

- Spread small amount of soup-bean mixture into sprayed 9 x 13-inch (23 x 33 cm) baking dish.

- Arrange half of tortilla strips over soup-bean mixture. Make 1 layer of chicken, another layer of half soup-bean mixture, remaining tortilla strips and remaining chicken. Top with remaining soup-bean mixture.

- Cover and bake for 45 minutes or until it bubbles.

- Uncover and spread shredded cheese over top of casserole. Return to oven for about 5 minutes until cheese melts. Serves 10.

Classic Chicken Marsala

5 - 6 boneless, skinless chicken
    breast halves
3 eggs, beaten
4 tablespoons oil   60 ml
Italian seasoned breadcrumbs
1 (1 pound) fresh mushrooms,
    sliced   455 g
2 - 3 cloves garlic, minced
1 (10 ounce) can chicken
    broth   280 g
½ cup marsala wine   125 ml
1 (4 ounce) package shredded
    mozzarella cheese   115 g

- Rinse chicken pieces, pat dry and flatten to about ¼-inch (6 mm) thick with rolling pin. Dip chicken in beaten eggs and coat all sides.

- Marinate covered in refrigerator for several hours or overnight. Turn chicken occasionally.

- When ready to bake, preheat oven to 350° (175°C).

- Heat oil in large skillet over medium-high heat. Dip chicken in breadcrumbs, place in skillet and brown on all sides. Drain and place in sprayed 9 x 13-inch (23 x 33 cm) baking dish.

- Spread mushrooms over chicken. Mix garlic, broth and wine in bowl and pour over chicken. Cover and bake for 30 minutes. Remove cover and bake for an additional 25 minutes.

- Sprinkle cheese over top of chicken pieces and bake for an additional 5 minutes or until cheese melts. Serves 10.

Chicken Tetrazzini

½ cup (1 stick) butter	115 g
6 tablespoons flour	45 g
2 (14 ounce) cans chicken broth	2 (400 g)
1 (8 ounce) carton whipping cream	250 ml
1 (16 ounce) package linguine, cooked, drained	455 g
5 - 6 boneless, skinless chicken breast halves, cooked, cubed	
1 cup sliced fresh mushrooms	70 g
2 ribs celery, chopped	
1 green bell pepper, chopped	
1 (4 ounce) jar diced pimentos, drained	115 g
4 - 5 drops hot sauce	
½ cup grated parmesan cheese	50 g

- Preheat oven to 350° (175° C).

- Melt butter in saucepan over medium heat, add flour, a little salt and pepper and stir until smooth. Gradually add broth and bring to boil. Cook and stir constantly until it thickens.

- Remove from heat and stir in cream. If sauce seems too thick, add a little milk.

- Mix 2 cups (500 ml) sauce with cooked linguine, pour into sprayed 9 x 13-inch (23 x 33 cm) baking dish and spread over baking dish.

- To remaining sauce, add chicken, mushrooms, celery, bell pepper, pimentos and hot sauce and mix well. Pour over linguine and sprinkle with parmesan cheese.

- Cover and bake for about 45 minutes. Uncover and bake for an additional 10 minutes. Serves 10.

TIP: *You may use leftover turkey instead of chicken as long as the turkey is not smoked turkey. The white meat of the turkey is better to use than the dark meat.*

Blue Ribbon Chicken

Chicken

3 large boneless, skinless chicken breast halves, cooked
1 (8 ounce) can mild taco sauce   230 g
Garlic powder
1 medium onion, chopped
1 (8 ounce) carton sour cream   230 g
1 cup white sauce (recipe below)
1 (7 ounce) package corn tortillas, torn   200 g
1½ cups shredded Monterey Jack cheese   360 ml
Sliced jalapenos
Chili powder

- Preheat oven to 350° (176° C).

- Shred chicken breasts and mix with taco sauce. Sprinkle with a little garlic powder, salt and pepper and set aside. Combine sour cream and white sauce (see next column) and set aside.

- Place half of tortillas in sprayed 9 x 13-inch (23 x 33 cm) baking dish. Add chicken mixture and half of sour cream mixture. Sprinkle with remaining tortillas.

- Top with remaining sour cream mixture and sprinkle with cheese. Scatter jalapenos and chili powder over top.

- Bake for 20 to 30 minutes or until it is thoroughly hot. Serves 6 to 8.

White Sauce:

2 tablespoons butter   30 ml
2 tablespoons flour   30 ml
1 cup milk, warmed   250 ml

- Melt butter in skillet over medium heat, add flour and stir constantly to mix well. (Make sure there are no lumps.) Heat and stir several minutes until paste-like mixture forms.

- Pour milk into mixture, stir constantly and bring to a boil. Reduce heat to simmer, continue to stir constantly and cook about 2 minutes. Stir in a little salt and pepper and remove from heat.

Chicken-Broccoli Casserole

8 boneless, skinless chicken breast halves, sliced	
½ cup (1 stick) butter	115 g
½ cup flour	60 g
2 cups half-and-half cream	500 ml
1 (14 ounce) can chicken broth	400 g
1 (8 ounce) package shredded cheddar cheese, divided	230 g
1 (3 ounce) package fresh grated parmesan cheese	85 g
2 tablespoons lemon juice	30 ml
1 tablespoon mustard	15 ml
2 tablespoons dried parsley	30 ml
1 tablespoon dried onion flakes	15 ml
3 tablespoons fresh chopped onion	30 g
¾ cup mayonnaise	170 g
2 (10 ounce) boxes frozen broccoli florets, slightly cooked	2 (280 g)
1 (7 ounce) package thin spaghetti	200 g

- Preheat oven to 350° (175° C).

- Wash chicken and dry well with paper towels. Melt butter in large saucepan or roasting pan and add flour.

- Add half-and-half cream and stir constantly over medium-low heat until thick. Add chicken broth, half cheddar cheese, parmesan cheese, lemon juice, ¼ teaspoon (1 ml) pepper, mustard, parsley, onion and 2 teaspoons (10 ml) salt.

- Heat on low until cheeses melt. Remove from heat and add mayonnaise. Add broccoli and chicken slices to sauce.

- Cook spaghetti according to package directions. Drain and pour into 10 x 15-inch (25 x 38 cm) glass dish. (This will not fit in 9 x 13-inch/ 23 x 33 cm glass dish.)

- Spread sauce and chicken mixture over spaghetti and sprinkle remaining cheese over top. Bake for 40 minutes. Serves 6 to 8.

Chicken-Ham Lasagna

1 (4 ounce) can chopped mushrooms, drained	115 g
1 large onion, chopped	
¼ cup (½ stick) butter	60 g
½ cup flour	30 g
Ground nutmeg	
1 (14 ounce) can chicken broth	400 g
1 (1 pint) half-and-half cream	500 ml
1 (3 ounce) package grated parmesan cheese	85 g
1 (16 ounce) package frozen broccoli florets	455 g
9 lasagna noodles, cooked, drained	
1½ cups cooked, finely diced ham, divided	210 g
2 cups cooked, shredded chicken breasts	280 g
1 (12 ounce) package shredded Monterey Jack cheese, divided	340 g

- Preheat oven to 350° (175° C).

- Saute mushrooms and onion in butter in large skillet. Stir in flour, 1 teaspoon (5 ml) salt and ¼ teaspoon (1 ml) pepper and a dash of nutmeg and stir until they blend well.

- Gradually stir in broth and half-and-half cream, cook and stir for about 2 minutes or until it thickens. Stir in parmesan cheese.

- Cut broccoli florets into smaller pieces and add to cream mixture. Discard stems.

- Spread about ½ cup (35 g) cream-broccoli mixture in sprayed 10 x 15-inch (25 x 38 cm) baking dish. Layer with 3 noodles, one-third of remaining broccoli mixture, ½ cup (70 g) ham, 1 cup (140 g) chicken and 1 cup (115 g) Monterey Jack cheese.

- Top with 3 more noodles, one-third of broccoli mixture, 1 cup (140 g) ham, 1 cup (140 g) chicken and 1 cup (115 g) Monterey Jack cheese. Pour in remaining noodles, chicken and cream-broccoli mixture.

- Cover and bake for 50 minutes or until it bubbles. Sprinkle with remaining cheese. Let stand for 15 minutes before cutting into squares to serve. Serves 12 to 14.

Chicken-Ham Tetrazzini

½ cup slivered almonds, toasted	85 g
1 (10 ounce) can cream of mushroom soup	280 g
1 (10 ounce) can cream of chicken soup	280 g
¾ cup milk	175 ml
2 tablespoons dry white wine	30 ml
1 (7 ounce) package spaghetti, cooked, drained	200 g
2½ cups cooked, diced chicken	350 g
2 cups cooked, diced ham	280 g
½ cup chopped green bell pepper	75 g
½ cup halved, pitted ripe olives	65 g
1 (8 ounce) package shredded cheddar cheese	230 g

- Preheat oven to 350° (175° C).

- Combine almonds, soups, milk and wine in bowl. Stir in spaghetti, chicken, ham, bell pepper and olives.

- Pour mixture into sprayed 9 x 13-inch (23 x 33 cm) baking dish. Sprinkle top of mixture with cheddar cheese and bake for 35 minutes or until hot and bubbly. Serves 8.

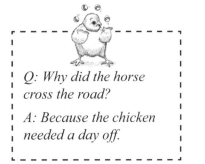

Q: Why did the horse cross the road?

A: Because the chicken needed a day off.

Chicken-Cheese Casserole

1 (10 ounce) can cream of
    chicken soup   280 g
3 cups cooked, chopped
    chicken or turkey   420 g
1 (16 ounce) package frozen
    broccoli florets, thawed   455 g
⅔ cup mayonnaise   150 g
1 cup shredded cheddar
    cheese   115 g
1½ cups crushed cheese
    crackers   90 g

- Preheat oven to 350° (175° C).

- Mix soup with ¼ cup (60 ml) water in large bowl. Add chicken, broccoli, mayonnaise and cheese and mix well.

- Pour into sprayed 3-quart (3 L) baking dish and spread cracker crumbs over top. Bake for 40 minutes. Serves 8.

Tootsie's Chicken Spectacular

This is a great recipe for leftover chicken or turkey.

2 cups cooked, diced chicken 280 g
1 (15 ounce) can green beans,
    drained   425 g
1 cup cooked white rice   165 g
1 (10 ounce) can cream of
    celery soup   280 g
½ cup mayonnaise   110 g
½ cup sliced water chestnuts 20 g
2 tablespoons chopped
    pimento   25 g
2 tablespoons chopped onion 20 g

- Preheat oven to 350° (175° C).

- Combine all ingredients with ¼ teaspoon (1 ml) salt and a dash of pepper in bowl and mix well.

- Place in 1½-quart (1.5 L) baking dish and bake for 25 to 30 minutes. Serves 8.

TIP: For a change, substitute cream of mushroom soup or cream of chicken soup.

Chicken-Noodle Delight

This recipe is a hearty main dish and the bell peppers make it colorful as well. It's a great family supper.

2 ribs celery, chopped	
½ onion, chopped	
½ green bell pepper, chopped	
½ red bell pepper, chopped	
6 tablespoons (¾ stick) butter, divided	85 g
3 cups cooked, cubed chicken breasts	420 g
1 (4 ounce) can sliced mushrooms, drained	115 g
1 (16 ounce) jar sun-dried tomato alfredo sauce	455 g
½ cup half-and-half cream	125 ml
1½ teaspoons chicken bouillon granules	7 ml
1 (8 ounce) package medium egg noodles, cooked, drained	230 g

- Preheat oven to 325° (160° C).

- Combine celery, onion, bell peppers and 4 tablespoons (55 g) butter in skillet or large saucepan and saute for about 5 minutes.

- Remove from heat and add chicken, mushrooms, alfredo sauce, half-and-half cream, chicken bouillon and noodles and mix well. Pour into sprayed 3-quart (3 L) baking dish.

Topping:

1 cup corn flake crumbs	30 g
½ cup shredded cheddar cheese	60 g

- Combine topping ingredients in bowl and sprinkle over casserole. Bake for 20 minutes or until casserole bubbles around edges. Serves 10.

Chicken-Orzo Florentine

4 boneless, skinless chicken
   breast halves
¾ cup orzo   70 g
1 (8 ounce) package fresh
   mushrooms, sliced   230 g
1 (10 ounce) package frozen
   spinach, thawed,
   well drained*   280 g
1 (10 ounce) can golden
   mushroom soup   280 g
½ cup mayonnaise   110 g
1 tablespoon lemon juice   15 ml
1 (8 ounce) package shredded
   Monterey Jack cheese,
   divided   230 g
½ cup seasoned Italian
   breadcrumbs   60 g

- Preheat oven to 350° (175° C).

- Cook chicken in boiling water for about 15 minutes and reserve broth. Cut chicken in bite-size pieces and set aside. Pour broth through strainer and cook orzo in remaining broth.

- Saute mushrooms in large, sprayed skillet until tender. Remove from heat and stir in chicken, orzo, spinach, soup, mayonnaise, lemon juice and ½ teaspoon (2 ml) pepper. Fold in half cheese and mix well.

- Spoon into sprayed 9 x 13-inch (23 x 33 cm) baking dish and sprinkle with remaining cheese and breadcrumbs. Bake for 35 minutes. Serves 8.

TIP: Squeeze spinach between paper towels to completely remove excess moisture.

Chicken-Sausage Extraordinaire

1 (6 ounce) box long grain-wild rice	170 g
1 pound pork sausage	455 g
1 cup chopped celery	100 g
2 onions, chopped	
1 (4 ounce) jar sliced mushrooms, drained	115 g
4 boneless, skinless, chicken breast halves, cooked, sliced	
¼ cup butter, divided	55 g
¼ cup flour	30 g
1 cup whipping cream	250 ml
1 (14 ounce) can chicken broth	400 g
1 teaspoon poultry seasoning	5 ml
2 cups crushed crackers	120 g

- Preheat oven to 350° (175° C).

- Cook rice according to package directions and set aside.

- Brown sausage in skillet and remove with slotted spoon. Saute celery and onions in sausage fat until onion is transparent, but not brown. Drain.

- Stir in mushrooms and chicken and set aside. Melt 3 tablespoons (35 g) butter in large saucepan, add flour and mix well.

- Slowly add cream, broth and poultry seasoning. Cook, stirring constantly over medium heat until mixture is fairly thick. Pour into large bowl.

- Add rice, sausage-onion mixture, chicken-mushroom mixture and ½ teaspoon (2 ml) each of salt and pepper. Spoon into sprayed 10 x 15-inch (25 x 38 cm) baking dish.

- Mix 1 tablespoon (15 ml) melted butter, crushed crackers in bowl and sprinkle over casserole. Bake for 40 minutes or until bubbles around edges. Serves 12 to 14.

TIP: *This dish makes enough for about 12 to 14 people so you could easily place into 2 smaller baking dishes and freeze one.*

Alfredo Chicken

**5 - 6 boneless, skinless
    chicken breast halves
Olive oil
1 (16 ounce) package frozen
    broccoli florets, thawed   455 g
1 red bell pepper, seeded,
    chopped
1 (16 ounce) jar alfredo
    sauce   455 g**

- Preheat oven to 325° (160° C).

- Brown and cook chicken breasts
  in large skillet with a little oil
  until juices run clear. Transfer
  to sprayed 9 x 13-inch
  (23 x 33 cm) baking dish.

- Microwave broccoli according
  to package directions and drain.
  Spoon broccoli and bell pepper
  over chicken.

- Heat alfredo sauce with
  ¼ cup (60 ml) water in small
  saucepan. Pour over chicken
  and vegetables. Cover and bake
  for 15 to 20 minutes. Serves 6.

*TIP: This chicken-broccoli dish can be
       "dressed up" a bit by sprinkling
       shredded parmesan cheese on top
       after casserole bakes.*

*Q: Why did the chicken
cross the road twice?*

*A: Because it was a
double-crosser.*

Chicken-Vegetable Medley

¼ cup (½ stick) plus 3 tablespoons butter	90 g
¼ cup flour	30 g
1 (1 pint) half-and-half cream	500 ml
½ cup cooking sherry	125 ml
1 (10 ounce) can cream of chicken soup	280 g
1 (10 ounce) package frozen broccoli spears, thawed	280 g
1 (10 ounce) package frozen cauliflower, thawed	280 g
1 red bell pepper, thinly sliced	
1 cup chopped celery	100 g
1 cup cooked brown rice	195 g
4 cups cooked, cubed chicken or turkey	560 g
1 (8 ounce) package shredded cheddar cheese	230 g
1 cup soft breadcrumbs	60 g

- Preheat oven to 350° (175° C).

- Melt ¼ cup (60 g) butter in saucepan, add flour and stir until they blend.

- Slowly stir in half-and-half cream and sherry and cook, stirring constantly until mixture thickens. Blend in soup until mixture is smooth and set aside.

- Place broccoli, cauliflower, red bell pepper and celery into sprayed 9 x 13-inch (23 x 33 cm) baking dish.

- Cover with rice, half sauce and top with chicken. Stir shredded cheese into remaining sauce and pour over chicken.

- Melt 3 tablespoons (35 g) butter and combine with breadcrumbs. Sprinkle over casserole. Bake for about 40 minutes or until casserole is thoroughly hot. Serves 12.

Chile-Chicken Casserole

3 boneless, skinless chicken
   breasts, cooked, cubed
1 bell pepper, chopped
1 onion, chopped
1 (4 ounce) can chopped
   green chilies, drained   115 g
1 teaspoon oregano   5 ml
1 teaspoon dried cilantro
   leaves   5 ml
½ teaspoon garlic powder   2 ml
1 (7 ounce) can whole green
   chilies, drained   200 g
1½ cups shredded Monterey
   Jack cheese   160 g
1½ cups shredded sharp
   cheddar cheese   160 g
3 large eggs
1 tablespoon flour   15 ml
1 cup half-and-half cream   250 ml

- Preheat oven to 350° (175° C).

- Combine chicken with bell pepper, onion, green chilies, oregano, cilantro, garlic powder, ½ teaspoon (2 ml) each of salt and pepper in skillet.

- Seed whole chilies and spread into sprayed 9 x 13-inch (23 x 33 cm) baking dish. Cover with meat mixture and sprinkle with cheeses.

- Combine eggs and flour in bowl and beat with fork until fluffy. Add half-and-half cream, mix well and pour over top of meat in baking dish. Bake for 30 to 35 minutes or until light brown. Serves 8.

Chinese Chicken

3½ cups cooked, cubed
  chicken 490 g
2 (10 ounce) cans cream
  of chicken soup 2 (280 g)
1 (16 ounce) can
  chop suey vegetables,
  drained 455 g
1 (8 ounce) can sliced
  water chestnuts,
  drained 230 g
¾ cup cashew nuts 105 g
1 cup chopped green
  bell peppers 150 g
1 bunch green onions
  with tops, sliced
½ cup chopped celery 50 g
⅓ teaspoon hot sauce 2 ml
¼ teaspoon curry
  powder 1 ml
1 (5 ounce) can chow
  mein noodles 145 g

- Preheat oven to 350° (175° C).

- Combine chicken, soups, vegetables, water chestnuts, cashew nuts, bell pepper, green onions, celery, hot sauce and curry powder in large bowl. Stir to mix well.

- Spoon mixture into sprayed 9 x 13-inch (23 x 33 cm) glass baking dish and sprinkle chow mein noodles over casserole.

- Bake for 30 to 35 minutes or until bubbly at edges. Set aside for about 5 minutes before serving. Serves 8.

Chinese Garden

It is stretching a point to call this Chinese, but the combination of ingredients makes a great tasting casserole.

1 (6 ounce) package fried rice with almonds and oriental seasoning	170 g
2 tablespoons butter	30 g
1 onion, chopped	
2 cups chopped celery	200 g
1 (15 ounce) can Chinese vegetables, drained	425 g
1 (8 ounce) can sliced bamboo shoots	230 g
3½ cups cooked, chopped chicken	490 g
1 (10 ounce) can cream of chicken soup	280 g
1 cup mayonnaise	225 g
2 tablespoons soy sauce	30 ml
½ teaspoon garlic powder	2 ml
1 cup chop mein noodles	55 g

- Preheat oven to 350° (175° C).

- Cook rice according to package directions and set aside.

- Heat butter in large skillet and saute onion and celery. Add Chinese vegetables, bamboo shoots and chicken and mix well.

- Heat chicken soup, mayonnaise, soy sauce, garlic powder and a little pepper in saucepan just enough to mix well.

- Combine rice, vegetable-chicken mixture and soup mixture in large bow land mix well. Transfer to sprayed 3-quart (3 L) baking dish.

- Sprinkle chow mein noodles over casserole. Bake for 35 minutes. Serves 8.

Comfort Chicken Plus

1 (6 ounce) box chicken stuffing mix	170 g
1 bunch fresh broccoli, cut into florets	
1 cup chopped celery	100 g
1 cup chopped red bell pepper	150 g
2 tablespoons butter	30 g
1 (8 ounce) can whole kernel corn, drained	230 g
2½ cups finely chopped chicken or leftover turkey	350 g
1 (1 ounce) packet hollandaise sauce mix	30 g
1 (3 ounce) can french-fried onions	85 g

- Preheat oven to 325° (160° C).

- Prepare chicken stuffing mix according to package directions.

- Place broccoli, celery, bell pepper, butter and ¼ cup (60 ml) water in microwave-safe bowl. Cover with wax paper and microwave on HIGH for 1½ minutes.

- Add broccoli-celery mixture, corn and chicken to stuffing and mix well. Spoon into sprayed 9 x 13-inch (23 x 33 cm) baking dish.

- Prepare hollandaise sauce according to package directions, but use 1¼ cups (310 ml) water instead of 1 cup (250 ml) water as directed.

- Pour hollandaise sauce over casserole and sprinkle top with onions. Bake for 25 minutes. Serves 8.

Creamed Chicken and Rice

4 cups cooked instant rice	380 g
6 tablespoons (¾ stick) butter, divided	85 g
¼ cup flour	30 g
2 cups milk	500 ml
2 teaspoons chicken bouillon granules	10 ml
1 teaspoon parsley flakes	5 ml
½ teaspoon celery salt	2 ml
4 cups cooked, cubed chicken	560 g
1 (16 ounce) package shredded Velveeta® cheese	455 g
1 (8 ounce) carton sour cream	230 g
1½ cups round, buttery cracker crumbs	90 g

- Preheat oven to 325° (160° C).

- Spread cooked rice into sprayed 9 x 13-inch (23 x 33 cm) baking dish and set aside.

- Melt 4 tablespoons (55 g) butter in large saucepan, stir in flour and mix until smooth. Gradually add milk, bouillon, seasonings and ½ teaspoon (2 ml) salt.

- Cook, stirring constantly, on medium heat for about 2 minutes or until sauce thickens.

- Reduce heat and add chicken, cheese and sour cream and stir until cheese melts.

- Spoon over rice in baking dish. Melt remaining 2 tablespoons (30 g) butter and toss with cracker crumbs. Sprinkle over casserole.

- Bake for 35 minutes or until hot. Serves 8.

Chicken Souffle

16 slices white bread, crusts
   removed
Butter, softened
5 boneless, skinless, chicken
   breast halves, cooked,
   thinly sliced diagonally
½ cup mayonnaise   110 g
1 cup shredded cheddar
   cheese, divided   110 g
5 large eggs
2 cups milk   500 ml
1 (10 ounce) can cream of
   mushroom soup   280 g

- Line 8 slices of bread, buttered on 1 side in sprayed 9 x 13-inch (23 x 33 cm) baking dish. Cover with sliced chicken.

- Spread chicken slices with mayonnaise and sprinkle with ½ cup (60 g) cheese. Top with remaining 8 slices bread.

- Beat eggs, milk, ½ teaspoon (2 ml) each of salt and pepper in bowl and pour over entire casserole. Refrigerate all day or overnight.

- When ready to bake, preheat oven to 350° (175° C). Spread mushroom soup with back of large spoon over top of casserole. Cover and bake for 45 minutes.

- Uncover, sprinkle with remaining cheddar cheese, return to oven and bake for an additional 15 minutes. Serves 8.

TIP: *You could use deli-sliced chicken instead of cooking chicken breasts to save time.*

Spicy Chicken-Enchilada Casserole

1 onion, chopped
2 tablespoons olive oil   30 ml
1 (15 ounce) can stewed
   tomatoes with juice   425 g
1 (8 ounce) can tomato
   sauce   230 g
1 (4 ounce) can chopped
   green chilies   115 g
1 (1 ounce) packet
   enchilada sauce mix   30 g
1 clove garlic, minced
3 - 4 cups cooked,
   shredded chicken   420 - 560 g
12 corn tortillas
1 (4 ounce) cans sliced
   black olives   115 g
1 (16 ounce) package
   shredded Monterey
   Jack cheese, divided   455 g

- Preheat oven to 350° (175° C).

- Saute onion with oil in large roasting pan until translucent, but not brown. Add tomatoes, tomato sauce, green chilies, enchilada sauce mix, garlic, ½ teaspoon (2 ml) salt and chicken. Bring to a boil, turn heat down and simmer for 15 minutes.

- Place 4 tortillas in sprayed 9 x 13-inch (23 x 33 cm) baking pan and spread evenly with one-third chicken mixture over top. Add one-third olives and 1 cup (110 g) cheese and spread evenly. Repeat layers twice, but reserve final layer of cheese.

- Cover and bake for 35 minutes. Uncover and sprinkle remaining cheese over top. Return to oven for 5 minutes. Serves 8 to 10.

Easy Chicken and Dumplings

**3 cups cooked, chopped
  chicken   420 g**
**2 (10 ounce) cans cream
  of chicken soup   2 (280 g)**
**3 teaspoons chicken
  bouillon granules   15 ml**
**1 (8 ounce) can
  refrigerated
  buttermilk biscuits   230 g**

- Combine chopped chicken, both cans of soup, chicken bouillon granules and 4½ cups (1.1 L) water in large soup pot or large, heavy pan. Boil mixture and stir to mix well.

- Separate biscuits and cut in half; cut again making 4 pieces out of each biscuit. Drop biscuit pieces, 1 at a time into boiling chicken mixture and stir gently.

- When all biscuits are in pot, reduce heat to low, simmer and stir occasionally for about 15 minutes. Serves 8.

TIP: Deli turkey will work just fine in this recipe. It's a great time-saver!

Family Chicken Bake

This is a great, basic "meat-and-potato" dish that all families love.

¼ cup (½ stick) butter	60 g
1 red bell pepper, chopped	
1 onion, chopped	
2 ribs celery, chopped	
1 (8 ounce) carton sour cream	230 g
1½ cups half-and-half cream	375 ml
1 (7 ounce) can chopped green chilies, drained	200 g
1 teaspoon chicken bouillon granules	5 ml
½ teaspoon celery salt	2 ml
3 - 4 cups cooked, cubed chicken	420 - 560 g
1 (16 ounce) package shredded cheddar cheese, divided	455 g
1 (2 pound) package frozen hash-brown potatoes, thawed	910 g

- Preheat oven to 350° (175° C).

- Melt butter in saucepan and saute bell pepper, onion and celery. Combine sour cream, half-and-half cream, green chilies, bouillon, celery salt, ½ teaspoon (2 ml) each of salt and pepper in large bowl.

- Stir in bell pepper mixture, chicken and half of cheese. Fold in hash-brown potatoes. Spoon into sprayed 9 x 13-inch (23 x 33 cm) baking dish.

- Bake for 45 minutes or until casserole is bubbly. Remove from oven and sprinkle remaining cheese over top of casserole. Return to oven for about 5 minutes. Serves 12 to 14.

TIP: For a change of pace, heat some hot, thick, chunky salsa to spoon over the top of each serving.

Family Night Spaghetti

This recipe has a little different twist on the ever-popular chicken spaghetti. This is a wonderful casserole to serve to family or for company. It has great flavor with chicken, pasta and colorful vegetables all in one dish. It's a real winner!

1 bunch fresh green onions with tops, chopped	
1 cup chopped celery	100 g
1 red bell pepper, chopped	
1 yellow or orange bell pepper, chopped	
¼ cup (½ stick) butter	60 g
1 tablespoon dried cilantro leaves	15 ml
1 teaspoon Italian seasoning	5 ml
1 (8 ounce) package thin spaghetti, cooked, drained	230 g
4 cups chopped, cooked chicken or turkey	560 g
1 (8 ounce) carton sour cream	230 g
1 (16 ounce) jar creamy alfredo sauce	455 g
1 (10 ounce) box frozen green peas, thawed	280 g
1 (8 ounce) package shredded mozzarella cheese, divided	230 g

- Preheat oven to 350° (175° C).

- Saute onions, celery and bell peppers in butter in large skillet. Combine onion-pepper mixture, cilantro, Italian seasoning, spaghetti, chicken, sour cream and alfredo sauce in large bowl and mix well.

- Sprinkle a little salt and pepper in mixture. Fold in peas and half mozzarella cheese. Spoon into sprayed 10 x 15-inch (25 x 38 cm) deep baking dish. Cover and bake for 45 minutes. Uncover and sprinkle remaining cheese over casserole. Return to oven for about 5 minutes. Serves 8 to 10.

TIP: If you want another twist, just use chopped, cooked ham instead of chicken.

Garden Chicken

This colorful, delicious casserole is not only flavor packed, but it is also a sight to behold! You can't beat this bountiful dish for family or company.

4 boneless, skinless chicken breasts halves, cut into strips	
1 teaspoon minced garlic	5 ml
6 tablespoons (¾ stick) butter, divided	85 g
1 small yellow squash, thinly sliced	
1 small zucchini, thinly sliced	
1 red bell pepper, thinly sliced	
4 tablespoons flour	30 g
2 teaspoons pesto seasoning	10 ml
1 (14 ounce) can chicken broth	400 g
1 cup half-and-half cream	250 ml
1 (8 ounce) package angel hair pasta, cooked al dente, drained	230 g
⅓ cup shredded parmesan cheese	35 g

- Preheat oven to 350° (175° C).

- Saute chicken and garlic in 3 tablespoons (35 g) butter in large skillet over medium heat for about 15 minutes. Remove ingredients and set aside.

- With butter that is left in skillet, saute squash, zucchini and bell pepper and cook just until tender-crisp.

- Melt 3 tablespoons (45 ml) butter in small saucepan and add flour, pesto seasoning and ½ teaspoon (2 ml) each of salt and pepper. Stir to form smooth paste.

- Gradually add broth, stirring constantly over medium-high heat, until thick. Stir in half-and-half cream and heat thoroughly.

- Combine chicken, vegetables, broth-cream mixture in large bowl and drained pasta. Transfer to sprayed 9 x 13-inch (23 x 33 cm) baking dish.

- Cover and bake for 30 minutes.

- Uncover and sprinkle parmesan cheese over top of casserole and return to oven for an additional 5 minutes. Serves 8.

Great Crazy Lasagna

*Chicken never got mixed up
with any better ingredients!*

1 tablespoon butter	15 ml
½ onion, chopped	
1 cup sliced fresh mushrooms	70 g
1 (10 ounce) can cream of chicken soup	280 g
1 (16 ounce) jar alfredo sauce	455 g
1 (4 ounce) jar diced pimentos, drained	115 g
⅓ cup dry white wine	75 ml
1 (10 ounce) package frozen chopped spinach, thawed	280 g
1 (15 ounce) carton ricotta cheese	425 g
⅓ cup grated parmesan cheese	35 g
1 egg, beaten	
9 lasagna noodles, cooked	
3 - 4 cups cooked, shredded chicken	420 - 560 g
1 (16 ounce) package shredded cheddar cheese, divided	455 g

- Preheat oven to 350° (175° C).

- Melt butter and saute onion and mushrooms in large skillet. Stir in soup, alfredo sauce, pimentos and wine. Reserve one-third sauce for top of lasagna.

- Squeeze spinach between paper towels to completely remove excess moisture. Combine spinach, ricotta, parmesan and egg in bowl and mix well.

- Place 3 noodles in sprayed 10 x 15-inch (25 x 38 cm) baking dish.

- Layer each with half of remaining sauce, spinach-ricotta mixture and chicken. (The spinach-ricotta mixture will be fairly dry.)

- Sprinkle with 1½ cups (171 g) cheddar cheese. Repeat layering. Top with last 3 noodles and reserved sauce.

- Cover and bake for 45 minutes. Uncover and sprinkle remaining cheese on top. Return to oven and bake for an additional 5 minutes. Let casserole stand for 10 minutes. Serves 12 to 14.

Green Chile-Chicken Enchilada Casserole

This classic casserole is good for all occasions. If you don't want to cook a whole chicken, use 6 to 8 boneless, skinless chicken breasts halves. It will save you some time.

1 whole chicken	
1 large onion, chopped	
3 ribs celery, chopped	
1 tablespoon butter	15 ml
1 (7 ounce) can chopped green chilies	200 g
1 cup milk	250 ml
1 (10 ounce) can cream of chicken soup	280 g
1 (10 ounce) can cream of mushroom soup	280 g
10 corn tortillas, cut into strips	
1 (12 ounce) package shredded cheddar cheese	340 g

- Preheat oven to 350° (175° C).

- Bake chicken in covered baking pan with 1½ cups (375 ml) water, onion, celery, butter, and a little salt and pepper for 1 hour or until juices run clear.

- Remove from oven, remove chicken to platter to cool and reserve 1 cup (250 ml) chicken stock. When chicken cools, remove meat from bone.

- Combine green chilies, milk, reserved chicken stock, chicken soup and mushroom soup in saucepan and heat just enough to mix.

- Place half of tortillas in sprayed 9 x 13-inch (23 x 33 cm) baking dish, cover with half chicken and half soup mixture and repeat layers.

- Cover and bake for about 30 minutes. Uncover and sprinkle cheese on top of casserole and bake for an additional 5 minutes. Serves 10.

Sizzling Chicken Pepe

2 (10 ounce) cans cream of chicken soup	2 (280) g
1 cup milk	250 ml
1 (1 ounce) packet taco seasoning	30 g
1 (4 ounce) can chopped green chilies	115 g
1 (10 ounce) package corn tortillas or chips	280 g
5 - 6 boneless, skinless chicken breasts, cooked, cubed	
1 (16 ounce) package shredded Monterey Jack cheese	455 g

- Preheat oven to 325° (160° C).

- Combine soups, milk, taco seasoning and green chilies in bowl.

- Make 2 layers of following ingredients in 9 x 13-inch (23 x 33 cm) glass baking dish: chips, chicken, soup mixture and cheese. Bake for 1 hour. Serves 6.

Q: Why did the chicken cross the road, roll in the mud and cross the road again?

A: Because he was a dirty double-crosser.

So Simple Chicken and Rice

4 - 6 boneless, skinless
    chicken breast halves
Seasoning salt
1 cup rice   95 g
1 (1 ounce) packet onion
    soup mix   30 g

- Preheat oven to 350° (175°C).

- Sprinkle chicken with seasoning salt and a little pepper. Place rice in sprayed 9 x 13-inch (23 x 33 cm) baking dish and place chicken on top.

- Mix 1½ cups (375 ml) water with onion soup mix and pour over chicken. Cover and bake for 1 hour 30 minutes. Serves 4 to 6.

Chicken-Cashew Bake

⅓ cup minced onion   55 g
1 cup minced celery   100 g
1 tablespoon butter, melted   15 ml
1 (10 ounce) can cream of
    mushroom soup   280 g
½ cup chicken broth   125 ml
1 tablespoon soy sauce   15 ml
3 drops hot sauce
2 cups cooked, diced chicken   280 g
1 cup chow mein noodles   55 g
½ cup chopped cashew nuts   70 g

- Preheat oven to 350° (175° C).

- Saute onion and celery in butter in saucepan. Add soup and chicken broth. Stir in soy sauce, hot sauce and chicken and simmer for about 5 minutes.

- Pour into 1-quart (1 L) baking dish. Sprinkle noodles and nuts on top.

- Bake for 20 minutes or until thoroughly hot. Serves 4 to 6.

Jazzy Turkey and Dressing

1 (8 ounce) package chicken stuffing mix	230 g
3 cups diced, cooked turkey	420 g
1 (15 ounce) can golden hominy, drained	425 g
1 (4 ounce) can chopped green chilies, drained	115 g
½ cup chopped red bell pepper	75 g
2 tablespoons dried parsley flakes	30 ml
1 (10 ounce) can cream of chicken soup	280 g
1 (8 ounce) carton sour cream	230 g
2 tablespoons butter, melted	30 g
2 teaspoons ground cumin	10 ml
1 cup shredded mozzarella cheese	115 g

- Preheat oven to 350° (175° C).

- Combine all ingredients in large mixing bowl except cheese with ½ cup (125 ml) water and ½ teaspoon (2 ml) salt and mix well.

- Pour into sprayed 9 x 13-inch (23 x 33 cm) baking dish. Cover and bake for 35 minutes.

- Uncover, sprinkle with cheese and bake for 5 minutes. Serves 10.

Jalapeno Chicken Bark

This one barks a little to get your attention, but it sure is good.

5 - 6 boneless, skinless
    chicken breast halves
¼ cup oil   **60 ml**
¼ cup white wine   **60 ml**
1 (1 pint) carton sour cream   **455 g**
1 tablespoon flour   **15 ml**
1 clove garlic, minced
½ teaspoon ground cumin   **2 ml**
1 (7 ounce) can whole
    jalapeno peppers   **200 g**
1 (12 ounce) package
    shredded Monterey
    Jack cheese   **340 g**
1 onion, sliced in rounds

- Preheat oven to 325° (160° C).

- Brown chicken on both sides in oil in skillet. Place in 9 x 13-inch (23 x 33 cm) baking dish.

- Combine wine, sour cream, flour, garlic, ½ teaspoon (2 ml) salt, ¼ teaspoon (1 ml) pepper, cumin and peppers in blender.

- Blend until smooth to make sauce. Pour sauce over chicken breasts, sprinkle with cheese and top with onion rings. Cover and bake for 1 hour. Serves 6.

TIP: *If you like it extra hot, leave the seeds in the jalapenos. If you take the seeds out, rubber gloves will protect your hands from the juices.*

Jalapeno Chicken

Even if you are not a spinach fan, you will find this to your liking!

2 cups chopped onion	320 g
2 tablespoons butter	30 g
1 (10 ounce) package frozen spinach, cooked, drained*	280 g
6 jalapenos or 1 (7 ounce) can green chilies, drained	200 g
1 (8 ounce) carton sour cream	225 g
2 (10 ounce) cans cream of chicken soup	2 (280 g)
4 green onions with tops, chopped	
1 (12 ounce) package corn tortilla chips, slightly crushed	340 g
4 cups cooked, diced turkey or chicken	560 g
1 (8 ounce) package shredded Monterey Jack cheese	230 g

- Preheat oven to 350° (175° C).

- Saute onion in butter in saucepan and blend in spinach, green chilies, sour cream, soups, onions and ½ teaspoon (2 ml) salt.

- Layer chips, chicken, spinach mixture and cheese in large 10 x 15-inch (25 x 38 cm) baking dish or two 9 x 9 inch (23 x 23 cm) dishes. Repeat process with cheese on top. Bake for 35 minutes. Serves 12.

TIP: Squeeze spinach between paper towels to completely remove excess moisture.

Jolly Ol' Chicken

With this casserole, you have the chicken and cranberry sauce all in one dish.

1 (6 ounce) package long grain-wild rice with seasonings	170 g
1 (16 ounce) can whole berry cranberry sauce	455 g
⅓ cup orange juice	75 ml
3 tablespoons butter, melted	35 g
½ teaspoon curry powder	2 ml
6 boneless, skinless chicken breast halves, cooked	
⅔ cup slivered almonds	110 g

- Preheat oven to 325° (160° C).

- Cook rice according to package directions and pour into sprayed 9 x 13-inch (23 x 33 cm) baking dish.

- Combine cranberry sauce, orange juice, butter and curry powder in saucepan and heat just enough to mix ingredients well.

- Place chicken breasts over rice and pour cranberry-orange juice mixture over chicken.

- Cover and bake for about 10 to 15 minutes.

- Uncover, sprinkle almonds over casserole and return to oven for about 10 to 15 minutes, just until chicken is light brown. Serves 8.

King Ranch Chicken

The King Ranch is the largest ranch in the U.S. and was established in 1852. Today the ranch covers more than 800,000 acres in South Texas with additional holdings in Brazil and three other states in the U.S.

8 (8 inch) corn tortillas, divided	8 (20 cm)
Chicken broth	
1 onion, chopped	
1 green bell pepper, chopped	
2 tablespoons butter	30 g
1 (10 ounce) can cream of chicken soup	280 g
1 (10 ounce) can cream of mushroom soup	280 g
1 tablespoon chili powder	15 ml
3 - 4 pound fryer, cooked, boned, diced	1.4 - 1.8 kg
1 (12 ounce) package shredded cheese	340 g
1 (10 ounce) can chopped tomatoes and green chilies	280 g

- Preheat oven to 350° (175° C).

- Dip half of tortillas in hot chicken broth just long enough to soften and place in sprayed 10 x 15-inch (25 x 38 cm) baking dish.

- Saute onion and bell pepper with butter in skillet. Stir in soups, chili powder and diced chicken.

- Pour layer of half soup-chicken mixture over tortillas and half cheese. Repeat layers and pour tomatoes and green chilies over casserole.

- Bake for 40 to 45 minutes or until hot and bubbly. Serves 12.

Don't Be Chicken Casserole

2 cups crushed tortilla chips	110 g
4 boneless, skinless chicken breast halves, cooked	
1 (15 ounce) can garbanzo beans, drained	425 g
1 (15 ounce) can pinto beans, drained	425 g
1 (15 ounce) can whole kernel corn, drained	425 g
1 (16 ounce) jar hot salsa	455 g
1 red onion, chopped	
2 teaspoons ground cumin	10 ml
1 teaspoon dried cilantro leaves	5 ml
1 green bell pepper, diced	
2 teaspoons minced garlic	10 ml
1 (8 ounce) package shredded Monterey Jack cheese, divided	230 g
1 (8 ounce) package shredded sharp cheddar cheese, divided	230 g

- Preheat oven to 350° (175° C).

- Scatter crushed tortilla chips evenly in sprayed 9 x 13-inch (23 x 343 cm) baking dish.

- Cut chicken breasts in thin slices. Combine chicken, beans, corn, salsa, onion, cumin, cilantro leaves, bell pepper, garlic and 1 teaspoon (5 ml) salt in large bowl and mix well.

- Spoon half of mixture evenly over chips.

- Combine cheeses in bowl and sprinkle half over mixture. Cover with remaining half of chicken-bean mixture and remaining cheese.

- Bake for 35 minutes. Let stand for 10 minutes before serving. Garnish with tomato slices, sour cream and chopped fresh onions, if you like. Serves 8 to 10.

Mexican-Turkey Fiesta

If you use leftover turkey, all you have to do to have a delicious casserole is to cut up your turkey, an onion and a bell pepper. The rest is opening cans and a bag of chips!

4 cups deli chopped turkey	560 g
1 onion, chopped	
1 (12 ounce) package shredded cheddar cheese	340 g
1 green bell pepper, chopped	
1 teaspoon chili powder	5 ml
½ teaspoon ground cumin	2 ml
2 (10 ounce) cans cream of chicken soup	2 (280 g)
1 (10 ounce) can diced green chilies and tomatoes	280 g
1 (13 ounce) bag tortilla chips	370 g

- Preheat oven to 325° (160° C).

- Combine all ingredients in large pan except tortilla chips. Add ½ teaspoon (2 ml) each of salt and pepper and mix well.

- Pour two-thirds tortilla chips into sprayed 9 x 13-inch (23 x 23 cm) baking dish and crush slightly with hands.

- Pour all turkey-cheese mixture over crushed tortilla chips and spread out. Crush remaining tortilla chips and spread over casserole. Bake for 40 minutes. Serves 10.

Not JUST Chicken

This is a great recipe for leftover ham or turkey. It is really a "quick fix" for the family.

3 cups cooked, cubed chicken or turkey	**420 g**
3 cups fully cooked, cubed ham	**420 g**
1 (8 ounce) package shredded cheddar cheese	**230 g**
1 (15 ounce) can English peas, drained	**425 g**
1 onion, chopped	
3 ribs celery, chopped	
¼ cup (½ stick) butter	**60 g**
⅓ cup plus 1 tablespoon flour	**45 g**
1 (1 pint) carton half-and-half cream	**500 ml**
½ cup milk	**125 ml**
1 teaspoon dill weed	**5 ml**
Instant brown rice, cooked	

- Preheat oven to 350° (175° C).

- Combine chicken, ham, cheese and English peas in large bowl.

- Saute onion and celery in butter in very large saucepan until tender. Add flour and stir to make a paste.

- Gradually add half-and-half cream, milk, dill weed and 1 teaspoon (5 ml) salt. Heat, stirring constantly, until mixture thickens.

- Add thickened cream mixture to chicken-ham mixture and mix well.

- Spoon into sprayed 4-quart (4 L) baking dish that you can take to the table.

- Cover and bake for 20 minutes. Spoon chicken and ham casserole over hot brown rice. Serves 12.

Old-Fashioned Chicken Spaghetti

This is a great recipe for leftover turkey.

8 - 10 ounces spaghetti	230 - 280 g
1 bell pepper, chopped	
1 onion, chopped	
1 cup chopped celery	100 g
½ cup (1 stick) butter	115 g
1 (10 ounce) can tomato soup	280 g
1 (10 ounce) can diced tomatoes and green chilies	280 g
1 (4 ounce) can chopped mushrooms	115 g
½ teaspoon garlic powder	2 ml
3 teaspoons chicken bouillon granules	15 ml
4 - 5 cups cooked, chopped chicken or turkey	560 - 700 g
1 (8 ounce) package cubed, Velveeta® cheese	230 g
1 (8 ounce) package shredded cheddar cheese	230 g

- Preheat oven to 325° (160° C).

- Cook spaghetti according to package directions and drain.

- Saute bell pepper, onion and celery in butter in medium saucepan.

- Add soup, tomatoes and green chilies, mushrooms, garlic powder, bouillon and ½ cup (125 ml) water and mix well.

- Mix spaghetti, soup, tomato mixture, chicken and cheeses in large mixing bowl. Place in sprayed 2 (2 quart/2 L) baking dishes.

- Cover and bake one dish for 40 to 50 minutes. Freeze the other dish for later. To cook frozen dish, thaw first. Serves 12.

Orange-Spiced Chicken

⅔ cup flour	80 g
½ teaspoon dried basil	2 ml
¼ teaspoon leaf tarragon	1 ml
2 - 3 tablespoons olive oil	30 - 45 ml
6 boneless, skinless, chicken breast halves	
1 (6 ounce) can frozen orange juice concentrate, thawed	170 g
½ cup white wine vinegar	125 ml
⅔ cup packed brown sugar	150 g
1 (6 ounce) box long grain-wild rice, cooked	170 g

- Preheat oven to 350° (175° C).

- Mix flour, 1 teaspoon (5 ml) salt, ½ teaspoon (2 ml) pepper and spices in resealable plastic bag. Pour oil into large skillet and heat. Coat chicken in flour mixture and brown both sides of chicken.

- Mix orange juice, ¼ cup (60 ml) water, vinegar and brown sugar in small bowl. When chicken breasts brown, place in sprayed 9 x 13-inch (23 x 33 cm) baking dish, cover with orange juice mixture and bake for 1 hour. Serve chicken and orange sauce over rice. Serves 6.

Poppy Seed Chicken

8 boneless, skinless chicken
  breast halves
1 (10 ounce) can cream of
  chicken soup   280 g
1 (8 ounce) carton sour
  cream   230 g
½ cup dry white wine or
  cooking wine   125 ml
1½ cups (1 stack) round
  buttery crackers   90 g
1 cup chopped almonds,
  toasted   85 g
½ cup (1 stick) butter,
  melted   115 g
2 - 3 tablespoons poppy
  seeds   20 - 25 g
Rice or noodles, cooked

- Preheat oven to 350° (175° C).

- Place chicken in sprayed
  9 x 13-inch (23 x 33 cm) baking
  pan and set aside.

- Combine soup, sour cream
  and wine in saucepan and heat
  just until it mixes. Pour soup
  mixture over chicken.

- Combine cracker crumbs,
  almonds and butter in bowl
  and sprinkle over casserole.
  Sprinkle with poppy seeds and
  bake for 45 minutes. Serve over
  rice or noodles. Serves 8.

Pollo Delicioso

4 fresh jalapeno chilies, seeded,
      diced
1 onion, chopped
1 bell pepper, chopped
1 clove garlic, minced
2 tablespoons oil   30 ml
1 teaspoon ground cumin   5 ml
½ teaspoon chili powder   2 ml
1 (10 ounce) can cream of
      chicken soup   280 g
1 (10 ounce) package frozen
      spinach, thawed   280 g
1 (1 pint) carton sour cream   455 g
4 large boneless, skinless
      chicken breasts halves,
      cooked, cubed
1 (13 ounce) package corn
      chips   370 g
1 (16 ounce) packages
      shredded Monterey
      Jack cheese   455 g

- Preheat oven to 325° (160° C).

- Saute chilies, onion, bell pepper and garlic in oil in large skillet. Stir in cumin, chili powder and chicken soup.

- Squeeze spinach between paper towels to completely remove excess moisture. Fold spinach, ½ teaspoon (2 ml) salt, sour cream and chicken into mixture. Heat, stirring constantly, but do not boil.

- Layer one-third corn chips, one-third cheese and one-half chicken mixture in sprayed 9 x 13-inch (23 x 33 cm) baking dish. Repeat layering and top with last layer of corn chips and cheese.

- Bake for 40 minutes or until casserole is hot and bubbly. Serves 10.

TIP: *Wear rubber gloves when removing seeds from jalapenos. If you like it hot, leave the seeds in.*

Pow Wow Chicken

3 onions, chopped
3 bell peppers, chopped
1 teaspoon garlic
    powder   5 ml
Olive oil
2 (10 ounce) cans
    chopped tomatoes
    and green
    chilies   2 (280 g)
1 (16 ounce) package
    cubed Velveeta®
    cheese   455 g
1 (12 ounce) package
    shredded cheddar
    cheese   340 g
6 cups cooked, chopped
    chicken   840 g
1 (1 pint) carton sour
    cream   455 g
1 (4 ounce) jar pimentos   115 g
Rice, cooked
Tortilla chips, crushed

- Cook onion, bell peppers and garlic in a little oil in skillet. Add tomatoes and green chilies and bring to boil. Reduce heat and simmer for about 15 to 20 minutes or until slightly thick.

- Add cheeses, stir constantly and heat slowly until cheeses melt. Add chicken, sour cream and pimentos. Heat until hot, but do not boil.

- To serve, place rice on individual plate and top with a few crushed chips. Spoon chicken-cheese mixture over rice and chips. Serve immediately. Serves 12.

Red Rock Taco Chicken

This is a great recipe for leftover chicken.

3 cups cooked, chopped chicken	420 g
1 (1 ounce) packet taco seasoning	30 g
1 cup white rice	95 g
2 cups chopped celery	200 g
1 red bell pepper, seeded, chopped	
2 (15 ounce) cans Mexican stewed tomatoes	2 (425 g)
1 (6 ounce) can fried onion rings	170 g

- Preheat oven to 325° (160° C).

- Combine cooked chicken, taco seasoning, rice, ½ cup (125 ml) water, celery, bell pepper and tomatoes in large bowl. Transfer to sprayed 9 x 13-inch (23 x 33 cm) baking dish.

- Cover and bake for 25 minutes, remove cover and sprinkle onion rings over casserole. Return to oven for 15 minutes. Serves 8.

Chicky Chicken with Red Peppers

1 (14 ounce) can chicken broth	400 g
1 (8 ounce) can whole kernel corn, drained	230 g
2 cups cooked, cubed chicken breasts	280 g
1 cup roasted red bell peppers	135 g
¼ cup pine nuts, toasted	30 g

- Preheat oven to 325° (160° C).

- Combine chicken broth, corn, chicken and roasted bell peppers in saucepan over medium-high heat. Cover and simmer for about 10 minutes.

- Spoon into sprayed 7 x 11-inch (18 x 28 cm) baking dish, top with pine nuts and bake for 15 minutes. Serves 6.

Sassy Chicken over Tex-Mex Corn

2 teaspoons garlic powder	10 ml
1 teaspoon ground cumin	5 ml
⅔ cup flour	80 g
4 boneless, skinless chicken breast halves	
Olive oil	

• Combine garlic powder, cumin, flour and ample salt in shallow bowl. Dip chicken in flour mixture and coat each side of chicken.

• Place a little oil in heavy skillet over medium-high heat. Cut each chicken breast in half lengthwise. Brown each piece on both sides, reduce heat and add 2 tablespoons (30 ml) water to skillet.

• Cover and simmer for 15 minutes. Transfer chicken to foil-lined baking pan and place in oven at 250° (120° C) to keep warm.

Tex-Mex Corn:

1 (10 ounce) can chicken broth	280 g
1½ cups hot salsa	395 g
1 (11 ounce) can Mexicorn®	310 g
1 cup instant rice	95 g

• Use same unwashed skillet, combine broth, salsa and corn and cook for about 10 minutes. Stir in rice and let stand for 10 minutes or until rice is tender.

• To serve, spoon Tex-Mex Corn on platter and place chicken breasts over corn. Serves 4.

Sour Cream Chicken Enchiladas

4 - 5 boneless, skinless
   chicken breast halves
1 onion, chopped
2 tablespoons butter   30 g
1 (4 ounce) can chopped
   green chilies   115 g
1 (12 ounce) package
   shredded cheddar
   cheese   340 g
2 teaspoons chili powder,
   divided   10 ml
2 (8 ounce) cartons sour
   cream, divided   2 (230 g)
10 - 12 flour tortillas
¼ cup flour   30 g
¼ cup (½ stick) butter,
   melted   60 g
1 (12 ounce) package
   shredded Monterey
   Jack cheese, divided   340 g

- Preheat oven to 350° (175° C).

- Cook chicken in enough water in saucepan to cover chicken, drain and reserve 1½ cups (375 g) broth. Allow chicken to cool and chop into small pieces.

- Saute onion in butter, add chicken, green chilies, cheddar cheese, 1 teaspoon (5 ml) chili powder and 1 cup (240 g) sour cream and mix well.

- Microwave tortillas on HIGH for about 1 minute or until softened. Spoon a little chicken-cheese mixture onto each tortilla and roll to enclose filling.

- Place seam-side down in sprayed 10 x 15-inch (25 x 38 cm) baking pan.

- Combine flour and melted butter in saucepan, mix well and add 1½ cups (375 ml) reserved broth. Cook, stirring constantly, until thick and bubbly.

- Fold in one-half cheese, remaining 1 cup (240 g) sour cream and remaining chili powder. Spoon over enchiladas.

- Bake for 30 minutes. Remove from oven and sprinkle with remaining cheese. Serves 12.

Chicken-Broccoli Deluxe

½ cup (1 stick) butter	115 g
½ cup flour	60 g
1 (14 ounce) can chicken broth	400 g
1 (1 pint) carton half-and-half cream	500 ml
1 (16 ounce) package shredded cheddar cheese, divided	455 g
1 (5 ounce) package grated parmesan cheese	145 g
2 tablespoons lemon juice	30 ml
2 tablespoons dried parsley	30 ml
¾ cup mayonnaise	170 g
2 (10 ounce) boxes frozen broccoli florets, slightly cooked	2 (280 g)
5 boneless, skinless chicken breast halves, cooked, sliced	
1 (12 ounce) box vermicelli	340 g

- Preheat oven to 325° (160° C).

- Melt butter in very large saucepan or roasting pan. Add flour and mix. Gradually add chicken broth and half-and-half cream, stirring constantly over medium-low heat until it thickens.

- Add half cheddar cheese, parmesan cheese, lemon juice dried parsley, 1 teaspoon (5 ml) salt and ½ teaspoon (2 ml) pepper. Heat on low until cheeses melt. Remove from heat and add mayonnaise.

- Punch small holes in broccoli boxes and microwave 4 minutes. Gently add broccoli and chicken slices to sauce.

- Cook vermicelli according to package directions, drain and pour into sprayed 10 x 15-inch (25 x 38 cm) baking dish. Spoon sauce and chicken mixture over vermicelli.

- Cover and bake for 40 minutes. Uncover and spread remaining cheese over top. Return to oven for an additional 5 minutes. Serves 12.

Eggcellent Chicken Pie

1 (12 ounce) package shredded cheddar cheese, divided	340 g
1 (10 ounce) package frozen, chopped broccoli, thawed	280 g
2 cups cooked, finely diced chicken breasts	280 g
½ cup finely chopped onion	80 g
½ cup finely chopped red bell pepper	75 g
1⅓ cups half-and-half cream	310 ml
3 eggs	
¾ cup baking mix	90 g

- Preheat oven to 375° (190° C).

- Combine 2 cups (230 g) cheddar cheese, broccoli, chicken, onion and bell pepper in bowl. Spread into sprayed 10-inch (25 cm) deep-dish pie pan.

- Beat half-and-half cream, eggs, baking mix and a little salt and pepper in bowl. Slowly pour cream-egg mixture over broccoli-chicken mixture, but do not stir.

- Cover and bake for 35 minutes. Uncover and sprinkle remaining cheese over top. Return to oven for about 5 minutes or just until cheese melts. Serves 8.

Q: What happens when you drop a hand gren-egg?

A: It egg-plodes.

Sour Cream Chicken Casserole

5 boneless, skinless chicken
    breast halves, cooked,
    cubed
1 (1 pint) carton sour
    cream   455 g
1 (7 ounce) package
    ready-cut spaghetti   200 g
2 (10 ounce) cans cream
    of chicken soup   2 (280 g)
1 (4 ounce) can
    mushrooms,
    drained   115 g
½ cup (1 stick) butter,
    melted   115 g
1 (5 ounce) package
    grated parmesan
    cheese   145 g

- Preheat oven to 325° (160° C).

- Combine all ingredients with ⅛ teaspoon (.5 ml) pepper in bowl.

- Pour into sprayed 9 x 13-inch (23 x 33 cm) baking dish. Sprinkle cheese on top. Cover and bake for 50 minutes. Serves 8.

Quickie Russian Chicken

This is great when you don't have time to cook.

6 boneless, skinless chicken
    breast halves
1 (8 ounce) bottle Russian
    salad dressing   250 ml
1 (12 ounce) jar apricot
    preserves   340 g
1 (1 ounce) packet onion
    soup mix   30 g

- Preheat oven to 350° (175° C).

- Place chicken breasts in sprayed 9 x 13-inch (23 x 33 cm) baking dish.

- Combine dressing, apricot preserves, onion soup mix and ¼ cup (60 ml) water in saucepan and bring to slow boil. Remove from heat and pour over chicken.

- Cover and bake for 1 hour. Uncover, baste with sauce and bake for an additional 30 minutes. Serves 6.

Spicy Orange Chicken over Noodles

1 pound boneless, skinless chicken tenders	455 g
2 tablespoons olive oil	30 ml
2 tablespoons soy sauce	30 ml
1 (16 ounce) package frozen stir-fry vegetables, thawed	455 g

- Lightly brown chicken tenders in oil in large skillet over medium-high heat. Add soy sauce and cook for an additional 3 minutes.

- Add stir-fry vegetables and cook for about 5 minutes or until vegetables are tender-crisp.

Sauce:

⅔ cup orange marmalade	215 g
1 tablespoon olive oil	15 ml
1 tablespoon soy sauce	15 ml
1½ teaspoons lime juice	7 ml
½ teaspoon minced ginger	2 ml
½ teaspoon cayenne pepper	2 ml
1 (6 ounce) package chow mein noodles	170 g

- Combine marmalade, oil, soy sauce, lime juice, minced ginger and cayenne pepper in saucepan and mix well.

- Heat and pour over stir-fry chicken and vegetables. Serve with chow mein noodles. Serves 8 to 10.

Stampede Chicken Enchiladas

This classic enchilada dish will make your herd excited. Get ready for the stampede.

3 cups cooked, shredded
   chicken   420 g
1 (4 ounce) can chopped
   green chilies   115 g
1 (7 ounce) can green chile
   salsa   200 g
1 onion, minced
6 chicken bouillon cubes
1 (1 pint) carton whipping
   cream   500 ml
Olive oil
10 corn tortillas
1 (12 ounce) package
   shredded Monterey
   Jack cheese   340 g
1 (8 ounce) carton sour
   cream   230 g

- Preheat oven to 350° (175° C).

- Combine chicken, green chilies, green chile salsa and onion in saucepan. Place bouillon cubes, ½ teaspoon (2 ml) salt and cream in saucepan and heat until bouillon dissolves, but do not boil.

- Heat oil in skillet and dip each tortilla into oil for about 5 seconds to soften. Drain on paper towels. Dip each tortilla into saucepan with cream and coat each side. Fill each tortilla with chicken mixture.

- Roll and place seam-side down in sprayed 9 x 13-inch (23 x 33 cm) baking dish. Pour remaining cream over enchiladas and sprinkle with cheese. Bake for 30 to 35 minutes. When ready to serve, top with dollops of sour cream. Serves 8.

Supper-Ready Chicken

You will have one skillet and one saucepan to wash. Within 20 minutes you will have creamy chicken plus vegetables ready to go in the oven. And the kids will love the crunchy topping.

6 boneless, skinless chicken breast halves	
2 tablespoons olive oil	**30 ml**
1 cup chopped celery	**100 g**
2 cups (½ inch thick) sliced zucchini	**250 g/1.2 cm**
1 (16 ounce) package baby carrots	**455 g**
½ onion, chopped	
¼ cup (½ stick) plus 2 tablespoons butter	**85 g**
1 (10 ounce) can cream of chicken soup	**280 g**
1 (10 ounce) can fiesta nacho cheese soup	**280 g**
1 cup milk or half-and-half cream	**250 ml**
½ teaspoon dill weed	**2 ml**
1 teaspoon dried basil	**5 ml**
1½ cups soft breadcrumbs	**90 g**
½ cup chopped walnuts	**45 g**

- Preheat oven to 375° (190° C).

- Brown chicken in skillet with oil. Place chicken breasts in sprayed 9 x 13-inch (23 x 33 cm) baking dish and set aside.

- Cook celery, zucchini, carrots and onion in saucepan for about 10 minutes in ¼ cup (60 g) butter and very little water and drain.

- Combine soups, milk, dill weed, basil and ½ teaspoon (2 ml) pepper in saucepan and heat just enough to mix well.

- Spoon about ¾ cup (175 ml) soup mixture over chicken. Combine remaining soup mixture with vegetables. Spoon over chicken and soup mixture.

- Combine 2 tablespoons (30 g) melted butter, breadcrumbs and walnuts in bowl and sprinkle over casserole. Bake for 35 to 40 minutes or until topping browns lightly. Serves 10.

Sweet-and-Sour Chicken and Veggies

1 (3 ounce) package chicken-flavored ramen noodles	85 g
1 (16 ounce) package frozen broccoli, cauliflower and carrots	455 g
3 boneless, skinless, chicken breast halves, cooked, cut in strips	
⅔ cup sweet-and-sour sauce	180 g
1 tablespoon soy sauce	15 ml

- Cook noodles and vegetables in 2 cups (500 ml) water (reserve seasoning packet) in large saucepan for 3 minutes or until liquid absorbs.

- Add seasoning packet, chicken (or turkey) sweet-and-sour sauce and soy sauce. Heat on medium-low heat, stirring until all is thoroughly hot. Serves 8 to 10.

Swiss Chicken

4 boneless, skinless chicken breast halves	
4 slices Swiss cheese	
1 (10 ounce) can cream of chicken soup	280 g
¼ cup dry white wine	60 ml
½ cup herb-seasoned chicken stuffing mix	20 g
¼ cup (½ stick) butter, melted	60 g

- Preheat oven to 350° (175° C).

- Arrange chicken in sprayed 9 x 13-inch (23 x 33 cm) pan. Top with cheese. Combine soup and wine in bowl and stir well.

- Spoon evenly over chicken and sprinkle with stuffing mix. Drizzle butter over crumbs. Bake for 45 to 55 minutes. Serves 4.

Sweet Pepper Chicken

6 - 8 boneless, skinless chicken
   breasts halves
2 tablespoons olive oil .... 30 ml
⅓ cup cornstarch .... 45 g
⅔ cup sugar .... 135 g
½ cup packed brown sugar ...... 110 g
1 teaspoon chicken bouillon
   granules .... 5 ml
1 (15 ounce) can pineapple
   chunks with juice .... 425 g
1½ cups orange juice .... 375 ml
½ cup vinegar .... 125 ml
¼ cup ketchup .... 70 g
2 tablespoons soy sauce .... 30 ml
¼ teaspoon ground ginger ...... 1 ml
1 red bell pepper, thinly
   sliced

- Preheat oven to 325° (160° C).

- Brown chicken breasts in large skillet with oil. Place in sprayed 10 x 15-inch (25 x 38 cm) baking dish.

- Combine cornstarch, sugar, brown sugar and bouillon granules in large saucepan and mix well.

- Drain pineapple and save juice. Add pineapple juice, orange juice, vinegar, ketchup, soy sauce and ginger to cornstarch mixture in saucepan and mix well.

- Cook on high heat, stirring constantly, until mixture thickens. Pour sauce over chicken breasts.

- Bake for 45 minutes.

- Remove from oven, add pineapple chunks and thinly sliced bell peppers and bake for an additional 15 minutes. Serves 12 to 14.

Tortilla-Chip Chicken

1 (10 ounce) package
　tortilla chips,
　divided　　　　　280 g
1 onion, chopped
3 ribs celery, chopped
1 (10 ounce) can cream
　of chicken soup　280 g
2 (10 ounce) cans
　tomatoes and green
　chilies　　　　　2 (280 g)
1 (16 ounce) package
　cubed Velveeta®
　cheese　　　　　455 g
4 - 5 boneless, skinless
　chicken breast halves,
　cooked, cubed

- Preheat oven to 350° (175° C).

- Place half chips in sprayed 9 x 13-inch (23 x 33 cm) baking dish, crush a few chips with your hand.

- Combine onion, celery, chicken soup, tomatoes and green chilies and cheese in large saucepan. Stir on medium heat until cheese melts. Add chicken and pour over chips.

- Crush remaining chips in resealable plastic bag with rolling pin. Sprinkle over chicken-cheese mixture.

- Bake for about 35 minutes or until bubbly around edges. Serves 10.

Chicken-Run Casserole

1 onion, chopped	
1 cup sliced celery	100 g
3 tablespoons butter	35 g
4 cups diced cooked chicken	460 g
1 (6 ounce) package long grain-wild rice, cooked	170 g
1 (10 ounce) can cream of celery soup	280 g
1 (10 ounce) can cream of chicken soup	280 g
1 (4 ounce) jar pimentos, drained	115 g
2 (15 ounce) cans French-style green beans, drained	2 (425 g)
1 cup slivered almonds	170 g
1 cup mayonnaise	225 g
2½ cups crushed potato chips	140 g

- Preheat oven to 350° (175° C).

- Saute onion and celery in butter in large saucepan. Add chicken, rice, soups, pimentos, green beans, almonds, mayonnaise, ½ teaspoon (2 ml) salt and 1 teaspoon (5 ml) pepper and heat enough to mix.

- Pour into sprayed 10 x 15-inch (25 x 38 cm) baking dish. (This recipe needs a very large baking dish.)

- Sprinkle crushed potato chips over casserole and bake for 35 minutes or until potato chips are light brown. Serves 12 to 14.

Cheesy, Cheesy Chicken

Cheese lovers dig in!
This is a real winner!

1 onion, chopped	
1 red bell pepper, chopped	
½ green bell pepper, chopped	
½ cup (1 stick) butter, divided	115 g
1 (10 ounce) can cream of chicken soup	280 g
1 (4 ounce) can sliced mushrooms	115 g
½ teaspoon dried cilantro	2 ml
½ teaspoon dried basil	2 ml
1 teaspoon celery salt	5 ml
½ teaspoon garlic pepper	2 ml
1 (8 ounce) package egg noodles, cooked al dente, drained	230 g
4 - 5 boneless, skinless chicken breast halves, cooked, cubed	
1 (15 ounce) carton ricotta cheese	425 g
1 (16 ounce) package shredded cheddar cheese	455 g
⅓ cup grated parmesan cheese	35 g
1 cup breadcrumbs	60 g

- Preheat oven to 350° (175° C).

- Saute onion and bell peppers with 5 tablespoons (75 g) butter in skillet. Remove from heat and stir in soup, mushrooms, cilantro, basil, celery salt, garlic pepper and a little salt.

- Combine noodles, chicken, cheeses and soup-mushroom mixture in large bowl. Mix well.

- Spoon into sprayed 9 x 13-inch (23 x 33 cm) baking dish.

- Melt 3 tablespoons (35 g) butter and combine with breadcrumbs in bowl. Sprinkle over casserole.

- Cover and bake for 45 minutes. Serves 10.

The Chicken Takes the Artichoke

6 boneless, skinless chicken breast halves	
7 tablespoons butter, divided	95 g
1 (14 ounce) jar water-packed artichoke hearts, drained	400 g
1 (8 ounce) can sliced water chestnuts, drained	230 g
¼ cup flour	30 g
⅛ teaspoon ground nutmeg	.5 ml
1 teaspoon dried thyme	5 ml
1 (14 ounce) can chicken broth	400 g
½ cup whipping cream	125 ml
1 cup shredded Swiss cheese	110 g
1 cup seasoned breadcrumbs	120 g

• Preheat oven to 350° (175° C).

• Brown chicken breasts in 2 tablespoons (30 g) butter in skillet. Place chicken breasts in sprayed 9 x 13-inch (23 x 33 cm) baking dish.

• Cut each artichoke heart in half and place artichokes and water chestnuts around chicken.

• Melt 3 tablespoons (35 g) butter in saucepan and stir in flour, ½ teaspoon (2 ml) pepper, nutmeg and thyme until smooth and mix well.

• Gradually stir in broth and cook on medium-high heat, stirring constantly, until broth thickens. Remove from heat and stir in cream and cheese.

• Blend until cheese melts and pour over chicken, artichokes and water chestnuts.

• Combine breadcrumbs and 2 tablespoons (30 g) melted butter in bowl and sprinkle over top of casserole. Bake for 35 minutes. Serves 8.

Three Cheers for Chicken

8 boneless, skinless chicken
  breast halves
6 tablespoons (¾ stick)
  butter   85 g
1 onion, chopped
½ bell pepper, chopped
1 (4 ounce) jar chopped
  pimentos, drained   115 g
1 cup rice   95 g
1 (10 ounce) can cream of
  chicken soup   280 g
1 (10 ounce) can cream of
  celery soup   280 g
1 (8 ounce) can sliced water
  chestnuts   230 g
1 cup shredded cheddar
  cheese   115 g

- Preheat oven to 350° (175° C).

- Salt and pepper chicken and place in sprayed 10 x 15-inch (25 x 38 cm) glass baking dish.

- Melt butter in medium saucepan and add onion, bell pepper, pimentos, rice, soups, 2 soup cans water and water chestnuts and pour over chicken.

- Cover and bake for 15 minutes, reduce temperature to 325° (160° C) and cook for an additional 1 hour. Add cheese 5 minutes before dish is done and return to oven for last 5 minutes. Serves 12 to 14.

Tomatillo-Chicken Enchiladas

2 (13 ounce) cans tomatillos, drained	2 (370 g)
1 (7 ounce) can chopped green chilies	200 g
6 tablespoons canola oil, divided	90 ml
1 onion, chopped	
1 clove garlic, minced	
1 (14 ounce) can chicken broth	400 g
12 corn tortillas	
3 cups shredded cooked chicken	420 g
1 (12 ounce) packages shredded Monterey Jack cheese, divided	340 g
1 (8 ounce) carton sour cream	230 g

- Preheat oven to 350° (175° C).

- Combine tomatillos and green chilies in blender and process. Heat 2 tablespoons (30 ml) oil, add onion and garlic in large skillet and cook until onion is translucent.

- Stir in puree and chicken broth. Simmer until sauce reduces to consistency of canned tomato sauce.

- In separate skillet, heat remaining oil and cook tortillas about 3 seconds on each side. Dip softened tortilla into tomatillo mixture. Lay sauced tortilla on plate. Place ¼ cup (35 g) chicken and 2 tablespoons (15 g) cheese across tortilla and roll to close.

- Place enchilada, seam-side down in 10 x 15-inch (25 x 38 cm) baking pan. Repeat until all tortillas are filled. Spoon remaining sauce over enchiladas.

- Cover and bake for about 35 minutes. Uncover and top with reserved cheese and bake for an additional 10 minutes. When ready to serve, top each enchilada with 1 spoonful sour cream. Serves 10.

Taco Casserole

1 (10 ounce) cream of mushroom soup	280 g
1 (10 ounce) can cream of chicken soup	280 g
1 cup milk	250 ml
1 (1 ounce) packet taco seasoning	30 g
1 onion, chopped	
1 (4 ounce) can chopped green chilies, drained	115 g
5 - 6 boneless, skinless chicken breast halves, cooked	
1 (16 ounce) bag corn tortillas	455 g
1 (16 ounce) package shredded Monterey Jack cheese	455 g

- Preheat oven to 325° (160° C).

- Combine soups, milk, taco seasoning, onion and green chilies in bowl. Cut chicken breasts into bite-size pieces.

- Layer one-half chips, half chicken, half soup mixture and half cheese in sprayed 9 x 13-inch (23 x 33 cm) glass dish. Repeat layers in same order. Cheese will be on top. Bake for 1 hour. Serves 8.

A chicken will lay bigger and stronger eggs if you change the lighting to make it think a day is 28 hours long.

Zesty Orange Chicken

½ cup white wine	125 ml
½ cup orange juice concentrate	125 ml
½ cup orange marmalade	160 g
½ teaspoon ground ginger	2 ml
½ teaspoon ground cinnamon	2 ml
1 chicken, quartered	
2 (11 ounce) cans mandarin oranges, drained	2 (310 g)
½ cup halved green grapes	75 g
1½ cups instant brown rice, cooked	280 g

- Preheat oven to 325° (160° C).

- Combine wine, orange juice concentrate, marmalade, ginger and cinnamon in sprayed 9 x 13-inch (23 x 33 cm) baking dish. Add chicken quarters and turn to coat chicken.

- Bake, basting occasionally for 40 minutes. Add oranges and grapes to dish during last 5 minutes of cooking.

- Serve over brown rice. Serves 10.

Easy Chicken Casserole

1 cup chopped celery	100 g
1 red bell pepper, seeded, chopped	
1 large onion, chopped	
3 tablespoons olive oil	45 ml
1 (3 - 4 pound) chicken, cooked, boned, chopped	1.4 - 1.8 kg
1 (8 ounce) box macaroni, cooked, drained	230 g
1 (10 ounce) cream of mushroom soup	280 g
1 (8 ounce) package shredded American cheese, divided	230 g

- Preheat oven to 350° (175° C).

- Saute celery, red pepper and onion in oil in skillet. Combine remaining ingredients except 1 cup (108 g) cheese and mix well.

- Spoon into sprayed 9 x 13-inch (23 x 33 cm) baking dish. Top with remaining 1 cup (108 g) cheese. Bake for 20 minutes or until cheese melts. Serves 6 to 8.

Adobe Chicken

2 cups cooked brown rice	390 g
1 (10 ounce) can chopped tomatoes and green chilies, drained	280 g
3 cups cooked, chopped chicken	420 g
1 (8 ounce) package shredded Monterey Jack cheese, divided	230 g

- Preheat oven to 325° (160° C).

- Combine rice, tomatoes and green chilies, chicken and half cheese.

- Spoon into sprayed 7 x 11-inch (18 x 28 cm) baking dish. Cover and bake for 30 minutes.

- Uncover, sprinkle with remaining cheese and return to oven for 5 minutes. Serves 6 to 8.

Gobble Gobble Casserole

1 (7 ounce) package herb-seasoned stuffing	200 g
1 cup whole cranberry sauce	280 g
1 (12 ounce) can turkey	340 g
1 (10 ounce) can turkey gravy	280 g

- Preheat oven to 375° (190° C).

- Prepare stuffing according to package directions.

- Combine prepared stuffing and cranberry sauce in medium bowl and set aside.

- Place turkey in sprayed 2-quart (2 L) baking dish. Pour gravy over turkey and spoon stuffing mixture over casserole.

- Bake for 15 to 20 minutes. Serves 8.

Gobbler Supreme

1 onion, chopped	
1 cup sliced celery	100 g
3 tablespoons butter	35 g
4 cups cooked, diced turkey	560 g
1 (6 ounce) package long grain-wild rice, cooked (without seasoning packet)	170 g
Seasoning packet in rice package	
2 (10 ounce) cans cream of chicken soup	2 (280 g)
1 (4 ounce) jar pimentos, drained	115 g
2 (15 ounce) cans French-style green beans, drained	2 (425 g)
1 cup slivered almonds	170 g
1 cup mayonnaise	225 g
2½ cups crushed potato chips	140 g

- Preheat oven to 350° (175° C).

- Saute onion and celery in butter in large saucepan.

- Add turkey, rice, seasoning packet, soup, pimentos, green beans, almonds, mayonnaise, ½ teaspoon (2 ml) salt and 1 teaspoon (5 ml) pepper and stir.

- Pour into sprayed 10 x 15-inch (25 x 38 cm) baking dish. (This needs a very large casserole dish.) Sprinkle crushed potato chips over casserole.

- Bake for 35 minutes or until potato chips brown slightly. Serves 12.

TIP: If you want to make in advance and freeze, add potato chips when ready to cook casserole.

Turkey Perky Dinner

1 (2 pound) lemon-garlic
   seasoned, turkey
   tenderloin   910 g

Vegetables and Gravy:

12 - 14 medium new (red)
   potatoes, halved
2 (14 ounce) cans chicken
   broth, divided   2 (400 g)
½ cup (1 stick) butter,
   divided   115 g
5 - 6 medium yellow
   squash, sliced
¼ cup cornstarch   30 g

- Preheat oven to 325° (160° C).

- Place turkey tenderloin in 9 x 13-inch (23 x 33 cm) baking dish lined with foil. Sprinkle lots of pepper over turkey and bake for 1 hour 30 minutes.

- After tenderloin cooks 1 hour 10 minutes, place new potatoes in large saucepan and add 1 can chicken broth and ¼ cup (60 g) butter. Cook for 15 to 20 minutes or until tender.

- While potatoes cook, place squash in second saucepan and add remaining can broth and remaining ¼ cup (60 g) butter. Cook for about 10 minutes or until squash is just barely tender.

- Place tenderloin on large platter and use slotted spoon to place potatoes and squash around sliced tenderloin.

- Combine cornstarch and about ½ cup (125 ml) cooking broth and mix well. Combine broth into 1 saucepan, bring to boil and stir in cornstarch mixture. Add about 1 teaspoon (5 ml) pepper (and salt if you like) and cook, stirring constantly until liquid thickens.

- Serve in gravy boat with tenderloin and vegetables. Serves 12.

Crispy Chicky Chicken

1 (6 ounce) box long grain-wild rice with herbs and seasonings	170 g
2 cups chopped celery	200 g
1 onion, chopped	
1 cup coarsely chopped walnuts	130 g
2 tablespoons butter	30 g
2 cups mayonnaise	450 g
1 (8 ounce) carton sour cream	230 g
1 tablespoon lemon juice	15 ml
4 cups cooked, cubed chicken	560 g
1 cup crushed potato chips	55 g
1 (3 ounce) can fried onion rings, crushed	85 g

- Preheat oven to 325° (160° C).

- Cook rice according to package directions.

- Lightly saute celery, onion and walnuts in butter in skillet. Add mayonnaise, sour cream, lemon juice, ¾ teaspoon (4 ml) salt and chicken and mix well.

- Fold in cooked rice and transfer to sprayed 9 x 13-inch (23 x 33 cm) baking dish.

- Combine potato chips and crushed onion rings in bowl and sprinkle over top of casserole.

- Bake for 25 minutes. Serves 10 to 12.

Tempting Chicken and Veggies

1½ pounds chicken breast tenderloins	680 g
½ cup (1 stick) butter, divided	115 g
1 (6 ounce) box fried rice with seasoning packet	170 g
⅛ teaspoon cayenne pepper	.5 ml
¼ cup chopped red bell pepper	40 g
1 (10 ounce) package frozen broccoli spears, thawed	280 g
1 (10 ounce) package frozen corn, thawed	280 g

- Preheat oven to 350° (175° C).

- Brown chicken tenderloins in about 3 tablespoons (35 g) butter in skillet. Remove chicken to large bowl.

- In same skillet, saute rice until light brown with remaining butter and spoon into bowl with chicken. Add 2½ cups (625 ml) water, cayenne pepper, bell pepper, broccoli spears and corn and mix well.

- Spoon into sprayed 9 x 13-inch (23 x 33 cm) baking dish. Cover and bake for 25 minutes or until rice and vegetables are tender. Serves 10.

A broody is a hen that has laid or contributed to a clutch of eggs and is now waiting for them to hatch.

Barnyard Bakes and Broils

From hearty to light, spicy to mild, these inventive chicken specialties will make you fly over the coop. Just add these wonderful ingredients together, put them in the oven – and stand back!

Barnyard Bakes and Broils Contents

Barnyard Bakes and Broils Contents

Apache Trail Drumsticks

⅔ cup fine, dry breadcrumbs	80 g
⅔ cup finely crushed corn chips	40 g
1 (1 ounce) packet taco seasoning mix	30 g
1 (16 ounce) jar taco sauce, divided	455 g
2 pounds chicken drumsticks, skinned	910 g

- Preheat oven to 375° (190° C).

- Combine breadcrumbs, crushed corn chips and dry taco seasoning mix in bowl. Place ½ cup (135 g) taco sauce in flat bowl.

- Dip drumsticks in taco sauce, one at a time, then dredge in crumb mixture. Discard taco sauce used for dipping.

- Place on sprayed 10 x 15-inch (25 x 38 cm) baking pan and bake for 30 to 35 minutes. Serve with remaining taco sauce. Serves 8.

Apricot-Ginger Chicken

2 teaspoons ground ginger	10 ml
½ cup Italian dressing	125 ml
4 boneless, skinless chicken breast halves	
⅔ cup apricot preserves	210 g

- Combine ginger and Italian dressing and place in large resealable plastic bag. Add chicken to bag, marinate in refrigerator overnight and turn occasionally.

- When ready to bake, preheat oven to 350° (175° C). Remove chicken and reserve ¼ cup (60 ml) marinade. Place chicken in shallow baking dish.

- Pour ¼ cup (60 ml) marinade in saucepan, bring to boil and cook for 1 minute. Remove from heat, stir in apricot preserves and set aside.

- Bake for 45 minutes and brush with marinade mixture last 10 minutes of cooking. Serves 4.

Aztec Creamy Salsa Chicken

6 boneless, skinless chicken
    breast halves
1 (1 ounce) packet taco
    seasoning mix   30 g
1 (16 ounce) jar salsa   455 g
1 (8 ounce) carton sour
    cream   230 g

- Preheat oven to 350° (175° C).

- Brown chicken breasts in skillet and transfer to sprayed 9 x 13-inch (23 x 33 cm) baking dish. Sprinkle taco seasoning over chicken and top with salsa.

- Cover and bake for 35 minutes.

- Remove chicken to serving plates. Add sour cream to juices in pan, stir well and microwave on HIGH for about 2 minutes. Stir pan juices and sour cream for sauce to serve over chicken. Serves 6.

Bacon-Wrapped Chicken

6 boneless, skinless chicken
    breast halves
1 (8 ounce) carton cream
    cheese with onion and
    chives   230 g
Butter
6 bacon strips

- Preheat oven to 375° (190° C).

- Flatten chicken to ½-inch (1.2 cm) thickness and spread 3 tablespoons (40 g) cream cheese over each piece.

- Dot with butter and sprinkle with a little salt, roll and wrap each with 1 bacon strip.

- Place seam-side down in sprayed 9 x 13-inch (23 x 33 cm) baking dish and bake for 40 to 45 minutes or until juices run clear.

- To brown, broil 6 inches (15 cm) from heat for about 3 minutes or until bacon is crisp. Serves 6.

Baked Chicken Poupon

2 tablespoons dijon-style
    mustard   30 g
2 tablespoons oil   30 ml
1 teaspoon garlic powder   5 ml
½ teaspoon Italian seasoning 2 ml
4 boneless, skinless chicken
    breast halves

- Preheat oven to 375° (190° C).

- Mix mustard, oil, garlic powder and seasoning in resealable plastic bag, add chicken breasts and marinate for 15 minutes.

- Place chicken in sprayed 9 x 13-inch (23 x 33 cm) baking pan.

- Bake for 35 minutes. Serves 4.

Easy Baked Chicken

6 boneless, skinless chicken
    breast halves
½ cup (1 stick) butter,
    melted   60 g
Cornbread stuffing mix with
    seasoning, crushed

- Preheat oven to 350° (175° C).

- Dip chicken breast in melted butter.

- Roll in cornbread stuffing mix to coat.

- Bake for 45 minutes. Serves 6.

Finger Lickin' BBQ Chicken

1 (2 pound) chicken, quartered	910 g
½ cup ketchup	135 g
¼ cup (½ stick) butter, melted	60 g
2 tablespoons sugar	25 g
1 tablespoon mustard	15 ml
½ teaspoon minced garlic	2 ml
¼ cup lemon juice	60 ml
¼ cup white vinegar	60 ml
¼ cup Worcestershire sauce	60 ml

Preheat oven to 325° (160° C).

- Sprinkle chicken quarters with a little salt and pepper and brown in skillet. Place in sprayed 9 x 13-inch (23 x 33 cm) baking pan.

- Combine ketchup, butter, sugar, mustard, garlic, lemon juice, vinegar and Worcestershire sauce in bowl. Pour over chicken, cover and bake for 50 minutes. Serves 4.

Best-Ever Turkey Loaf

2 pounds ground turkey	910 g
1 (6 ounce) package stuffing mix for beef plus seasoning packet	170 g
2 eggs, beaten	
½ cup ketchup, divided	135 g

- Preheat oven to 350° (175° C).

- Combine ground turkey, stuffing mix, eggs and ¼ cup (70 g) ketchup in bowl and mix well.

- Shape meat in oval loaf into center of sprayed 9 x 13-inch (23 x 33 cm) baking dish.

- Spread remaining ¼ cup (70 g) ketchup on top of loaf.

- Bake for 1 hour. Serves 8.

Catalina Chicken

6 boneless, skinless chicken
    breast halves
1 (8 ounce) bottle Catalina
    dressing   **230 g**
1½ cups crushed cracker
    crumbs   **90 g**

- Preheat oven to 350° (175° C).

- Marinate chicken breasts in Catalina dressing for 3 to 4 hours and discard marinade. Combine 1 teaspoon (5 ml) pepper and cracker crumbs.

- Dip each chicken breast in crumbs and place in sprayed 9 x 13-inch (23 x 33 cm) baking dish.

- Bake for 1 hour. Serves 6 to 8.

Cheesy Crusted Chicken

¾ cup mayonnaise (not light)   **170 g**
½ cup grated parmesan
    cheese   **50 g**
5 - 6 boneless, skinless chicken
    breast halves
1 cup Italian breadcrumbs   **120 g**

- Preheat oven to 375° (190° C).

- Combine mayonnaise and cheese in bowl. Place chicken breasts on sheet of wax paper and spread mayonnaise-cheese mixture over chicken. Sprinkle heavily with dry breadcrumbs on both sides.

- Place chicken on sprayed 9 x 13-inch (23 x 33 cm) baking pan so pieces do not touch.

- Bake for 20 minutes (25 minutes if chicken pieces are fairly large). Chicken pieces can be sliced and placed on serving platter. Serves 6.

Chicken and Beef Collide

1 (4 ounce) jar sliced dried beef, slices separated	115 g
6 strips bacon	
6 boneless, skinless chicken breast halves	
1 (10 ounce) can cream of chicken soup	280 g

- Preheat oven to 325° (160° C).

- Place dried beef in sprayed 9 x 13-inch (23 x 33 cm) baking dish. Wrap bacon strip around each chicken breast and place over beef.

- Heat chicken soup and ¼ cup (60 ml) water in saucepan and pour over chicken.

- Cover and bake for 1 hour. Serves 6.

Chicken Crunch

4 - 6 boneless, skinless chicken breast halves	
½ cup Italian salad dressing	125 ml
½ cup sour cream	120 g
2½ cups crushed corn flakes	70 g

- Place chicken in resealable plastic bag and add salad dressing and sour cream. Seal and refrigerate 1 hour. Remove chicken from marinade and discard marinade.

- When ready to bake, preheat oven to 375° (190° C).

- Dredge chicken in corn flakes and place in sprayed 9 x 13-inch (23 x 33 cm) baking dish.

- Bake for 45 minutes. Serves 4 to 6.

Parmesan Chicken Breasts

6 boneless, skinless chicken
   breast halves
1½ cups dry breadcrumbs   180 g
½ cup grated parmesan
   cheese   50 g
1 teaspoon dried basil   5 ml
½ teaspoon garlic powder   2 ml
1 (8 ounce) carton sour
   cream   230 g

- Preheat oven to 325° (160° C).

- Flatten chicken to ½-inch
  (1.2 cm) thickness. Combine
  breadcrumbs, parmesan cheese,
  basil and garlic powder in
  shallow dish.

- Dip chicken in sour cream, coat
  with crumb mixture and place
  (so chicken breasts do not touch)
  in sprayed 10 x 15-inch
  (25 x 38 cm) baking dish.

- Bake for 50 to 60 minutes or
  until golden brown. Serves 6.

Chicken Diablo

6 boneless, skinless chicken
   breast halves
1 (8 ounce) package cream
   cheese, softened   230 g
1 (16 ounce) jar salsa   455 g
2 teaspoons ground cumin   10 ml
1 bunch fresh green onions
   with tops, chopped

- Preheat oven to 350° (175° C).

- Pound chicken breasts to flatten.
  Beat cream cheese in bowl
  until smooth; add salsa, cumin
  and onions.

- Place heaping spoonful of cream
  cheese mixture on each chicken
  breast and roll. (There will be
  leftover cream cheese mixture.)

- Place in sprayed 7 x 11-inch
  (18 x 28 cm) baking dish.
  Spoon remaining cream cheese
  mixture over chicken rolls.
  Cover and bake for 30 minutes,
  uncover and continue cooking
  until chicken rolls are light
  brown. Serves 6.

Chicken Dipping

1½ cups cornbread stuffing
    mix with seasoning
    packet   55 g
¼ cup olive oil   60 ml
4 boneless, skinless chicken
    breast halves
Dipping sauce

- Preheat oven to 350° (175° C).

- Place stuffing mix in resealable plastic bag and crush with rolling pin.

- Add oil to center of 9 x 13-inch (23 x 33 cm) baking pan and spread around entire pan.

- Cut chicken breasts into 3 or 4 pieces, dip in stuffing mix and place in baking pan. Arrange chicken in pan without touching.

- Bake for 25 minutes. Remove from oven, turn pieces over and bake for an additional 15 minutes or until brown.

Dipping Sauce:

¼ cup honey   60 ml
3 tablespoons spicy brown
    mustard   45 g

- Combine honey and mustard in bowl and mix well. Dip chicken in dipping sauce and enjoy. Serves 4.

Q: Why did the chicken cross the basketball court?

A: He heard the referee calling fowls.

Chicken Oriental

1 (6 ounce) jar sweet-and-
   sour sauce   170 g
1 (1 ounce) packet onion
   soup mix   30 g
1 (16 ounce) can whole
   cranberry sauce   455 g
6 boneless, skinless chicken
   breast halves

- Preheat oven to 325° (160° C).

- Combine sweet-and-sour sauce, onion soup mix and cranberry sauce in bowl.

- Place chicken breasts in sprayed 9 x 13-inch (23 x 33 cm) shallow baking dish. Pour cranberry mixture over chicken breasts.

- Cover and bake for 30 minutes. Uncover and bake for an additional 25 minutes. Serves 6 to 8.

Chicken Parmesan

1½ cups biscuit mix   180 g
⅔ cup grated parmesan
   cheese   70 g
6 boneless, skinless chicken
   breast halves
½ cup (1 stick) butter,
   melted   115 g

- Preheat oven to 325° (160° C).

- Combine biscuit mix and parmesan cheese in shallow bowl.

- Dip chicken in butter and in biscuit-cheese mixture.

- Place in sprayed 9 x 13-inch (23 x 33 cm) baking dish. Bake for 1 hour or until light brown. Serves 6 to 8.

Chicken Parmesan and Spaghetti

1 (14 ounce) package frozen, cooked, breaded, chicken cutlets, thawed	400 g
1 (28 ounce) jar spaghetti sauce	795 g
2 (5 ounce) packages grated parmesan cheese, divided	2 (145 g)
1 (8 ounce) package thin spaghetti, cooked	230 g

- Preheat oven to 375° (190° C).

- Place cutlets in sprayed 9 x 13-inch (23 x 33 cm) baking dish and top each with about ¼ cup (65 g) spaghetti sauce and 1 heaping tablespoon (15 ml) parmesan. Bake for 15 minutes.

- Place cooked spaghetti on serving platter and top with cutlets. Sprinkle remaining cheese over cutlets. Heat remaining spaghetti sauce and serve with chicken and spaghetti. Serves 8.

Apricot Chicken

1 cup apricot preserves	320 g
1 (8 ounce) bottle Catalina dressing	230 g
1 (1 ounce) packet onion soup mix	30 g
6 boneless, skinless chicken breast halves	
Rice, cooked	

- Preheat oven to 325° (160° C).

- Combine apricot preserves, dressing and soup mix in bowl.

- Place chicken breasts in sprayed 9 x 13-inch (23 x 33 cm) baking dish and pour apricot mixture over chicken.

- Bake for 1 hour 20 minutes. Serve over rice. Serves 6 to 8.

TIP: For a change of pace, use Russian dressing instead of Catalina.

Chicken Breast Eden Isle

1 (8 ounce) carton sour cream	230 g
1 (3 ounce) cream cheese, softened	85 g
1 (10 ounce) can cream of chicken soup	280 g
1 (2.5 ounce) jar dried beef	70 g
6 boneless, skinless chicken breast halves	
6 bacon strips	
Rice, cooked	

- Preheat oven to 325° (160° C).

- Beat sour cream, cream cheese and soup in bowl. Line bottom of baking dish with dried beef. Place chicken breasts, wrapped with bacon strips onto dried beef.

- Spoon sour cream mixture over chicken. Cover and bake for 2 hours. Uncover last few minutes to brown. Serve over rice. Serves 6.

Chicken Pockets

1 (3 ounce) package cream cheese, softened	85 g
3 tablespoons butter, softened	35 g
1 (12 ounce) can chicken	340 g
2 tablespoons milk	30 ml
1 tablespoon chopped chives	15 ml
1 (8 ounce) can crescent rolls	230 g
Parmesan cheese	
Breadcrumbs	

- Preheat oven to 350° (175° C).

- Combine cream cheese with butter in bowl until smooth. Add chicken, milk and chives plus ⅛ teaspoon (.5 ml) salt.

- Separate dough into 4 rectangles and press seams together.

- Spoon mixture into center of dough. Pull 4 corners up and twist together. Seal sides by pinching together.

- Sprinkle top with parmesan cheese and breadcrumbs. Bake on baking sheet for 20 to 25 minutes. Serves 8.

Fruited Chicken

**6 large boneless, skinless
   chicken breast halves**
**½ cup (1 stick) butter,
   melted**   **115 g**
⅔ cup flour   **80 g**
Paprika
**1 (15 ounce) can chunky
   fruit cocktail with juice   425 g**

- Preheat oven to 350° (175° C).

- Dip chicken in butter and flour. Place in sprayed 9 x 13-inch (23 x 33 cm) baking dish. Sprinkle with a little salt, pepper and paprika.

- Bake for 45 minutes.

- Pour fruit and half juice over chicken. Bake for an additional 20 minutes. Serves 6.

Chicken Pot Pie

**1 (15 ounce) package
   refrigerated piecrust   425 g**
**1 (19 ounce) can cream of
   chicken soup   540 g**
**2 cups diced cooked chicken
   breasts   280 g**
**1 (10 ounce) package frozen
   mixed vegetables,
   thawed   280 g**

- Preheat oven to 325° (160° C).

- Line 1 layer piecrust in 9-inch (23 cm) deep-dish pie pan. Fill with chicken soup, chicken and mixed vegetables. Gently stir to mix.

- Cover with second layer of piecrust, fold edges under and crimp. With knife, cut 4 slits in center of piecrust. Bake for 1 hour 15 minutes or until crust is golden brown. Serves 8.

TIP: *When you're too busy to cook a chicken, get rotisserie chicken from the grocery store. They are great.*

Chicken Quesadillas

**3 boneless, skinless chicken
   breast halves, cubed
1 (10 ounce) can cheddar
   cheese soup   280 g
⅔ cup chunky salsa   175 g
10 flour tortillas**

- Preheat oven to 400° (205° C).

- Cook chicken in skillet until juices evaporate and stir often. Add soup and salsa and heat thoroughly.

- Spread about ⅓ cup (75 ml) soup mixture on half tortilla to within ½-inch (1.2 cm) of edge. Moisten edge with water, fold over and seal. Place tortillas on 2 baking sheets.

- Bake for 5 to 6 minutes. Serves 8.

Barnyard Supper

**5 boneless, skinless chicken
   breast halves
5 slices onion
5 potatoes, peeled,
   quartered
1 (10 ounce) can cream of
   celery soup   280 g**

- Preheat oven to 325° (160° C).

- Place chicken breasts in sprayed 9 x 13-inch (23 x 33 cm) baking dish. Top chicken with onion slices and place potatoes around chicken.

- Heat soup with ¼ cup (60 ml) water in saucepan just enough to pour soup over chicken and vegetables.

- Cover and bake for 1 hour 10 minutes. Serves 5.

Chicken Salsa

Chicken:

6 boneless, skinless chicken
    breast halves
1 tablespoon cornstarch   15 ml

Marinade:

1 (16 ounce) jar salsa	455 g
¾ cup honey	255 g
½ cup light soy sauce	125 ml
2 tablespoons oil	30 ml
½ teaspoon dried ginger	2 ml

- Wash and dry each chicken piece with paper towels.

- Combine all marinade ingredients in bowl and mix well. Pour 1½ cups (375 ml) marinade into resealable plastic bag, add chicken and refrigerate 2 to 3 hours. Cover and refrigerate remaining marinade.

- When ready to bake, preheat oven to 350° (175° C). Place drained chicken (discard chicken marinade) in sprayed 9 x 13-inch (23 x 33 cm) baking dish. Top with remaining refrigerated marinade and bake for 25 to 30 minutes or until juices run clear.

- Remove chicken and keep warm. Combine cornstarch with 2 tablespoons (30 ml) water in small saucepan and stir in pan juices.

- Bring to a boil and cook for about 2 minutes, stirring constantly until it thickens.

- To serve, pour sauce over chicken. Serves 6.

Chicken Scarborough Fair

For best results, make early in the day and refrigerate or prepare 1 hour before serving.

6 boneless, skinless chicken breast halves	
½ cup (1 stick) butter, softened, divided	**115 g**
3 slices mozzarella cheese	
1 egg, beaten	
½ cup flour	**60 g**
1 cup seasoned breadcrumbs	**120 g**
2 tablespoons chopped parsley	**30 ml**
¼ teaspoon dried sage	**1 ml**
¼ teaspoon rosemary	**1 ml**
¼ teaspoon thyme	**1 ml**
½ cup dry white wine	**125 ml**

- Flatten chicken breasts between sheets of wax paper and spread half of butter over each piece. Season with a little salt and pepper and place 1 slice cheese on each piece.

- Roll chicken with ends tucked in. Beat egg with 1 tablespoon (15 ml) water. Coat chicken lightly with flour, dip in egg and roll in breadcrumbs. Arrange rolls seam-side down in sprayed 7 x 11-inch (18 x 28 cm) baking dish and refrigerate for 1 hour.

- When ready to bake, preheat oven to 350° (175° C).

- Remove from refrigerator, melt remaining butter and add parsley, sage, rosemary and thyme in saucepan. Cover and bake for 30 minutes and baste with butter mixture.

- Remove from oven and pour wine over chicken. Bake for an additional 20 minutes and baste with pan juices. Serves 6.

Chicken-Broccoli Bake

2 bags Success white rice	
1 (8 ounce) package cubed Velveeta® cheese	230 g
1 (16 ounce) package frozen broccoli florets, thawed	455 g
3 cups cooked, cubed chicken or turkey	420 g
1 cup cracker or breadcrumbs	60 g

- Preheat oven to 325° (160° C).

- Cook rice in large saucepan according to package directions. Stir in cheese and ¼ cup (60 ml) water, stir and mix until cheese melts.

- Cook broccoli according to package directions. Add broccoli and chicken to rice-cheese mixture and mix well.

- Spoon into sprayed 9 x 13-inch (23 x 33 cm) baking dish. Top with cracker or seasoned breadcrumbs and bake for 15 minutes. Serves 8.

Chip Chicken

2 cups crushed potato chips	110 g
¼ teaspoon garlic powder	2 ml
5 - 6 boneless, skinless chicken breast halves	
½ cup (1 stick) butter, melted	115 g

- Preheat oven to 350° (175° C).

- Combine potato chips and garlic powder in bowl and mix well.

- Dip chicken breasts in butter and roll in potato chip mixture.

- Place in sprayed shallow baking dish and bake for 55 minutes. Serves 6.

Chicken-Cheese Enchiladas

1 (1 ounce) packet taco
    seasoning   30 g
2 tablespoons olive oil,
    divided   30 ml
4 - 5 large boneless,
    skinless chicken
    breast halves, cubed
1 (16 ounce) jar chunky
    salsa, divided   455 g
1 (12 ounce) package
    shredded Monterey
    Jack cheese,
    divided   340 g
1 (15 ounce) carton
    ricotta cheese   425 g
1 (4 ounce) can chopped
    green chilies   115 g
1 egg
1 teaspoon dried
    cilantro   5 ml
10 (8 inch) flour
    tortillas   10 (20 cm)
Sour cream

- Combine ¼ cup (60 ml) water, taco seasoning and 1 tablespoon (15 ml) oil in shallow bowl and mix well. Place seasoning mixture in resealable plastic bag. Add chicken, seal and refrigerate for 1 to 2 hours.

- When ready to bake, preheat oven to 350° (175° C).

- Cook chicken in remaining oil in skillet over medium-high heat for about 15 minutes.

- Combine ½ cup (65 g) salsa and ¼ cup (60 ml) water and spoon into sprayed

- 9 x 13-inch (23 x 33 cm) baking dish. Spread evenly over bottom of dish.

- Combine 2½ cups (285 g) Monterey Jack cheese, ricotta cheese, green chilies, egg, cilantro and ½ teaspoon (2 ml) salt in bowl.

- Spoon ⅓ cup (40 g) cheese mixture down center of each tortilla, top with chicken and roll. Place tortillas seam-side down over salsa mixture in dish.

- Drizzle remaining salsa over enchiladas and sprinkle with remaining cheese.

- Bake for 25 minutes. To serve, top with a dab of sour cream. Serves 6 to 8.

Almond-Crusted Chicken

1 egg
¼ cup seasoned
    breadcrumbs   60 ml
1 cup sliced almonds   190 g
4 boneless, skinless chicken
    breast halves
1 (5 ounce) package grated
    parmesan cheese   145 g

- Preheat oven to 325° (160° C).

- Place egg and 1 teaspoon (5 ml) water in shallow bowl and beat.

- In separate shallow bowl, combine breadcrumbs and almonds. Dip each chicken breast in egg, then in almond mixture and place in sprayed 9 x 13-inch (23 x 33 cm) baking pan.

- Bake for 20 minutes. Remove chicken from oven and sprinkle parmesan cheese over each breast. Bake for an additional 15 minutes or until almonds and cheese are golden brown.

Sauce:

1 teaspoon minced garlic   5 ml
⅓ cup finely chopped onion   55 g
2 tablespoons oil   30 ml
1 cup white wine   250 ml
¼ cup teriyaki sauce   60 ml

- Saute garlic and onion in oil in saucepan.

- Add wine and teriyaki sauce and bring to a boil. Reduce heat and simmer for about 10 minutes or until mixture reduces by half.

- When serving, divide sauce among 4 plates and place chicken breasts on top. Serves 4.

Chicken-Taco Bake

12 tortillas
Olive oil
1 onion, chopped
2 tablespoons butter   30 g
2 cups tomato juice   500 ml
1 (4 ounce) can chopped
   green chilies   115 g
1 (12 ounce) package
   shredded cheddar
   cheese   340 g
1 (8 ounce) carton
   whipping cream   250 ml
5 boneless, skinless chicken
   breast halves, boiled,
   cubed

- Preheat oven to 350° (175° C).

- Quarter tortillas and fry in oil in skillet until crisp. Drain and set aside.

- Saute onion in butter in skillet, add tomato juice, ½ teaspoon (2 ml) each of salt and pepper and green chilies. Simmer for 30 minutes.

- Add cheese, cream and chicken and heat until cheese melts.

- Alternate layers of chicken-cheese mixture and tortillas in sprayed 9 x 13-inch (23 x 33 cm) baking dish.

- Bake for 30 to 35 minutes. Serves 8.

An egg starts growing into a chick when it reaches a temperature of 86 degrees.

Chile-Chicken Roll-Ups

**8 boneless, skinless chicken
  breast halves**
**2 (4 ounce) cans diced
  green chilies   2 (115 g)**
**1 (8 ounce) package
  shredded cheddar
  cheese   230 g**
**½ cup (1 stick) butter,
  melted   115 g**
**2 cups crushed tortilla
  chips   110 g**

- Place each chicken breast on wax paper, flatten to about ¼-inch (6 mm) thickness with rolling pin or mallet and season with 1 teaspoon (5 ml) salt and ½ teaspoon (2 ml) pepper.

- Place green chilies and a little cheese evenly in center of each chicken breast. Carefully roll each chicken breast so no chilies or cheese seep out and secure with toothpicks.

- Place each chicken in small baking dish and refrigerate for several hours or overnight.

- When ready to bake, preheat oven to 350° (175° C). Roll each chicken breast in melted butter and crushed tortilla chips.

- Bake for about 25 to 30 minutes or until tender. Serves 8.

Chilly Night's Turkey Bake

1 (6 ounce) package stuffing mix for chicken, divided	170 g
1½ pounds deli turkey	680 g
1 (10 ounce) can cream of chicken soup	280 g
½ cup sour cream	120 g
1 (16 ounce) bag frozen mixed vegetables, thawed, drained	455 g

- Preheat oven to 375° (190° C).

- Sprinkle ½ cup (18 g) dry stuffing mix evenly in sprayed 9 x 13-inch (23 x 33 cm) baking dish. Set aside.

- Combine remaining stuffing and 1 cup (250 ml) water in bowl and stir just until moist. Set aside.

- Slice turkey into 1-inch (2.5 cm) strips and place over dry stuffing mix in baking dish. Mix soup, sour cream and vegetables in bowl, spoon over turkey strips and top with prepared stuffing. Bake for 25 minutes. Serves 8.

At the grocery store, select red meat and poultry last.

Lemon-Chicken Breeze

4 - 6 frozen, boneless,
   skinless chicken
   breast halves

½ cup (1 stick) butter	115 g
2 - 3 tablespoons oil	30 - 45 ml
2 - 3 tablespoons flour	15 - 25 ml
½ cup dry white wine	125 ml
¼ cup lemon juice	60 ml
4 tablespoons chopped parsley	60 ml

- Preheat oven to 350° (175°C).

- While chicken is slightly frozen, slice each breast into 3 thin slices. Melt butter in skillet with oil, dredge chicken in flour and brown on all sides. Drain chicken on paper towels.

- Add wine, lemon juice, parsley and a little salt and pepper to skillet and mix.

- Place chicken breasts in sprayed 9 x 13-inch (23 x 33 cm) baking dish and pour lemon mixture over chicken.

- Bake for 15 minutes or until sauce seeps into chicken. Serves 4 to 6.

Q: Why did the rubber chicken cross the road?

A: She wanted to stretch her legs.

Snazzy Chicken

**4 boneless, skinless chicken
    breast halves**
¼ cup lime juice   **60 ml**
**1 (.4 ounce) packet Italian
    salad dressing mix**   **10 g**
**¼ cup (½ stick) butter,
    melted**   **60 g**

- Preheat oven to 325° (160° C).

- Season chicken with a little salt
  and pepper and place in sprayed
  7 x 11-inch (18 x 28 cm)
  baking dish.

- Mix lime juice, salad dressing
  and melted butter in bowl and
  pour over chicken.

- Cover and bake for 1 hour.
  Remove cover for last
  15 minutes of cooking
  time. Serves 4.

Cola Chicken

**4 - 6 boneless, skinless
    chicken breast halves**
1 cup ketchup   **270 g**
1 cup cola   **250 ml**
**2 tablespoons
    Worcestershire sauce**   **30 ml**

- Preheat oven to 350° (175° C).

- Place chicken in sprayed
  9 x 13-inch (23 x 33 cm) baking
  dish and sprinkle with a little
  salt and pepper.

- Mix ketchup, cola and
  Worcestershire sauce in bowl
  and pour over chicken.

- Cover and bake for 50 minutes.
  Serves 6.

Cilantro-Chicken Breasts

6 boneless, skinless chicken breast halves	
3 teaspoons snipped cilantro, divided	15 ml
1¼ teaspoons ground cumin, divided	6 ml
2 cups breadcrumbs	120 g
Olive oil	
3 tablespoons butter	35 g
¼ cup flour	30 g
2 cups milk	500 ml
⅓ cup dry white wine	75 ml
1 (8 ounce) shredded Monterey Jack cheese	230 g

- Preheat oven to 350° (175° C).

- Pound chicken breast halves to ¼-inch (6 mm) thick with mallet or rolling pin.

- Mix 1 teaspoon (5 ml) each of salt and pepper, 2 teaspoons (10 ml) cilantro and 1 teaspoon (5 ml) cumin. Sprinkle seasonings over chicken cutlets and dip in breadcrumbs.

- Heat oil in large skillet and brown chicken on both sides. Remove to sprayed 9 x 13-inch (23 x 33 cm) baking dish.

- Melt butter in saucepan, blend in flour, ½ teaspoon (2 ml) salt, 1 teaspoon (5 ml) cilantro and ¼ teaspoon (1 ml) cumin in saucepan. Add milk, stir constantly and cook until sauce thickens.

- Remove from heat and stir in wine. Pour sauce over chicken. Cover and bake for 45 minutes.

- Remove from oven, sprinkle cheese on top of each piece of chicken and return to oven for 5 minutes. Serves 6.

Chile Pepper Chicken

5 boneless, skinless chicken
    breast halves
1 (1 ounce) packet
    hot-and-spicy
    coating mixture   30 g
1 (4 ounce) can chopped
    green chilies   115 g
Chunky salsa

- Preheat oven to 375° (190° C).

- Dredge chicken in coating mixture and place in sprayed 9 x 13-inch (23 x 33 cm) baking dish.

- Bake for 25 minutes.

- Remove from oven, spread green chilies over 5 chicken breasts and return to oven for 5 minutes. Serve with salsa over each chicken breast. Serves 5.

Company's Coming Chicken

2 chickens, quartered
2 (10 ounce) cans cream
    of mushroom soup   2 (280 g)
1 (1 pint) carton sour
    cream   455 g
1 cup sherry   250 ml
Rice, cooked

- Preheat oven to 300° (150° C).

- Place chickens in large shallow baking dish.

- Combine soup, sour cream and sherry in saucepan. Pour mixture over chicken.

- Cover and bake for 1 hour 15 minutes. Serve over rice. Serves 8 to 10.

TIP: *A little paprika on top makes this dish look great.*

Cranberry-Glazed Cornish Hens

6 cornish hens, thawed
1 (16 ounce) can whole
cranberry sauce   **455 g**
¼ cup (½ stick) butter   **60 g**
¼ cup frozen orange juice
concentrate   **60 ml**
2 teaspoons grated orange
peel   **10 ml**

- Preheat oven to 375° (190° C).

- Wash hens and pat dry with paper towels. Season inside and out with a little salt and pepper. Place hens in shallow pan without rack and bake for 35 minutes.

- Heat cranberry sauce, butter, orange juice and orange peel in saucepan. Pour mixture over hens.

- Lower temperature to 325° (160° C) and continue to bake for an additional 30 minutes. Baste often with cranberry sauce until it browns well. Serves 6.

Creamy Chicken Bake

1 (8 ounce) package egg noodles	230 g
1 (16 ounce) package frozen broccoli florets, thawed, trimmed	455 g
¼ cup (½ stick) butter, melted	60 g
1 (8 ounce) package shredded cheddar cheese	230 g
1 (10 ounce) can cream of chicken soup	280 g
1 cup half-and-half cream	250 ml
¼ teaspoon ground mustard	1 ml
3 cups cooked, cubed chicken breasts	420 g
⅔ cup slivered almonds	110 g

- Preheat oven to 325° (160° C).

- Cook noodles according to package directions, drain and keep warm.

- Combine noodles and broccoli in large bowl. Add butter and cheese and stir until cheese melts.

- Stir in chicken soup, half-and-half cream, mustard, chicken and 1 teaspoon (5 ml) each of salt and pepper. Spoon into sprayed 3-quart (3 L) baking dish.

- Cover and bake for about 25 minutes. Remove from oven, sprinkle with slivered almonds and cook for an additional 15 minutes. Serves 10.

Creamy Turkey Enchiladas

1 onion, finely chopped	
3 green onions with tops, chopped	
2 tablespoons butter	30 g
½ teaspoon garlic powder	2 ml
1 (7 ounce) can chopped green chilies, drained	200 g
2 (8 ounce) packages cream cheese, softened	2 (230 g)
3 cups cooked, diced turkey or chicken	420 g
8 (8 inch) flour tortillas	8 (20 cm)
2 (8 ounce) cartons whipping cream	2 (250 ml)
1 (16 ounce) package shredded Monterey Jack cheese	455 g

- Preheat oven to 350° (175° C).

- Saute onions in butter in large skillet.

- Add garlic powder, ½ teaspoon (2 ml) salt and green chilies and stir in cream cheese. Heat, stir until cream cheese melts and add diced turkey.

- Lay out 8 tortillas and spoon about 3 heaping tablespoons (45 ml) turkey mixture on each tortilla. Roll tortillas and place seam-side down in sprayed 9 x 13-inch (23 x 33 cm) baking dish.

- Pour whipping cream over enchiladas and sprinkle cheese over enchiladas. Bake for 35 minutes. Serves 8.

Crispy Herb-Seasoned Chicken

Marinade:
2 cups buttermilk*   **500 ml**
1 (2½ - 3 pound)
   chicken cut
   into quarters   **1.1 - 1.4 kg**

- Place buttermilk in large plastic container with lid and add chicken quarters and turn several times to coat.

- Marinate in buttermilk in refrigerator for 8 hours. Discard marinade.

Stuffing Mixture:

1 (9 ounce) package
   herb-seasoned
   stuffing mix   **255 g**
¼ cup grated parmesan
   cheese   **25 g**
½ teaspoon cayenne pepper   **2 ml**
½ cup (1 stick) butter,
   melted   **115 g**

- Preheat oven to 350° (175° C).

- Process stuffing mix, parmesan cheese and cayenne pepper in food processor until they blend well.

- Dip chicken pieces in melted butter and roll in stuffing mixture until they coat well.

- Place chicken on sprayed 9 x 13-inch (23 x 33 cm) baking sheet and bake for 1 hour 10 minutes. Serves 6 to 8.

*TIP: To make buttermilk, mix 1 cup (250 ml) milk with 1 tablespoon (15 ml) lemon juice or vinegar and let milk rest about 10 minutes.

Cranberry Chicken

6 boneless, skinless chicken
   breast halves
1 (16 ounce) can whole berry
   cranberry sauce   455 g
1 large tart apple, peeled,
   chopped
⅓ cup chopped walnuts   45 g
1 teaspoon curry powder   5 ml

- Preheat oven to 350° (175° C).

- Place chicken in sprayed
  9 x 13-inch (23 x 33 cm) baking
  pan and bake for 20 minutes.

- Combine cranberry sauce, apple,
  walnuts and curry powder in
  bowl and spoon over chicken.

- Bake for an additional 25
  minutes or until chicken juices
  run clear. Serves 6.

Crispy Nutty Chicken

⅓ cup minced dry-roasted
   peanuts   50 g
1 cup corn flake crumbs   30 g
½ cup ranch-style,
   buttermilk salad
   dressing   125 ml
6 boneless, skinless chicken
   breast halves

- Preheat oven to 350° (175° C).

- Combine peanuts and corn flake
  crumbs on wax paper. Pour
  dressing into pie pan, dip each
  piece of chicken in dressing and
  roll chicken in crumb mixture
  to coat.

- Arrange chicken in sprayed
  9 x 13-inch (23 x 33 cm) baking
  dish. Bake for 50 minutes or
  until light brown. Serves 6.

Glazed Drumsticks

1 (20 ounce) package frozen chicken drumsticks   **570 g**

- Preheat broiler. Place drumsticks in a single layer in sprayed 9 x 13-inch

- (23 x 33 cm) baking dish and broil for 10 minutes. Turn drumsticks and broil for an additional 10 minutes.

Sauce:

½ cup hoisin sauce	**135 g**
2 tablespoons light soy sauce	**30 ml**
1 teaspoon minced garlic	**5 ml**

- Preheat oven to 325° (160° C).

- Combine hoisin sauce, soy sauce and garlic in bowl and mix well. Brush chicken drumsticks lightly with sauce and bake for 25 minutes.

- During baking time, remove from oven and brush with remaining sauce. Continue cooking until glaze bubbles and browns. Serves 8.

Q: Why did the chicken go to the seance?

A: To get to the other side.

EZ Chicken

**6 boneless, skinless chicken
  breast halves**
**1 (10 ounce) can cream of
  chicken soup**   **280 g**
**1 (3 ounce) package cream
  cheese**   **85 g**
**1 (8 ounce) carton sour
  cream**   **230 g**
Lemon pepper
2 cups instant rice, cooked **330 g**

- Preheat oven to 300° (150° C).

- Place chicken breasts in shallow
  9 x 13-inch (23 x 33 cm)
  baking dish.

- Combine soup, cream cheese
  and sour cream in saucepan and
  heat on low just until cream
  cheese melts and ingredients
  mix well.

- Pour soup mixture over chicken
  breasts and sprinkle with lemon
  pepper. Cover and bake for
  1 hour.

- Uncover, bake for an additional
  15 minutes and serve over rice.
  Serves 8.

*Q: Why do hens
lay eggs?*

*A: If they drop them,
they'll break.*

Curry-Glazed Chicken

3 tablespoons butter	35 g
⅓ cup honey	115 g
2 tablespoons dijon-style mustard	30 g
1½ teaspoons curry powder	7 ml
4 boneless, skinless chicken breast halves	
2 cups instant rice, cooked	330 g

- Preheat oven to 375° (190° C).

- Melt butter in 9 x 13-inch (23 x 33 cm) baking pan.

- Mix honey, mustard and curry powder in pan with butter.

- Add chicken to pan and turn until chicken coats with butter mixture.

- Bake for 50 minutes, baste twice and serve over rice. Serves 4.

Easy Oven Chicken

One step does all!

6 tablespoons (¾ stick) butter	85 g
1 cup rice	95 g
1 (1 ounce) packet onion soup mix	30 g
1 cup chopped celery	100 g
1 (14 ounce) can chicken broth	400 g
1 (10 ounce) can cream of chicken soup	280 g
8 boneless, skinless chicken breast halves	

- Preheat oven to 325° (160° C).

- Melt butter in 9 x 13-inch (23 x 33 cm) glass baking dish. Add all remaining ingredients, except chicken and 2 cups (500 ml) water.

- Lay chicken breasts in rice and liquid mixture and cover with foil. Bake for 1 hour 10 minutes. Serves 5.

El Pronto Chicken

⅔ cup seasoned breadcrumbs	80 g
½ cup grated parmesan cheese	50 g
½ teaspoon garlic powder	2 ml
4 boneless, skinless chicken breast halves	
½ cup (1 stick) butter, melted	115 g
Rice, cooked	

- Preheat oven to 350° (175° C).

- Combine breadcrumbs and cheese with garlic powder, and salt and pepper in bowl and mix well.

- Dip chicken in butter, roll in breadcrumb mixture and place in sprayed 9 x 13-inch (23 x 33 cm) baking dish.

- Cover and bake for 55 minutes. Serve over rice. Serves 4.

Elegant Chicken

3 cups cooked shredded chicken	420 g
1 (6 ounce) package long grain-wild rice, cooked	170 g
1 (10 ounce) can cream of celery soup	280 g
1 (4 ounce) jar pimentos	115 g
1 cup mayonnaise	225 g
1 (15 ounce) can French-style green beans, drained	425 g
1 (2.8 ounce) can fried onion rings	85 g

- Preheat oven to 350° (175° C).

- Combine all ingredients in bowl except onion rings.

- Pour into sprayed 3-quart (3 L) baking dish. Bake for 15 to 20 minutes.

- Top with onion rings and cook for an additional 10 minutes. Serves 12.

Family-Secret Chicken and Noodles

This is a great recipe to prepare ahead of time and freeze.

¼ cup (½ stick) butter	60 g
½ cup flour	60 g
½ teaspoon basil	2 ml
½ teaspoon parsley	2 ml
2 cups milk	500 ml
1 (4 ounce) can sliced mushrooms, drained	115 g
1 (10 ounce) can cream of mushroom soup	280 g
1 (2 ounce) jar diced pimentos	60 g
1 (2 pounds) boneless, skinless chicken breast halves, cooked, diced	910 g
1 (14 ounce) can chicken broth	400 g
1 (16 ounce) package medium egg noodles	455 g
1 cup shredded cheddar or American cheese	115 g

- Melt butter in saucepan over medium heat and add flour, seasonings and ½ teaspoon (2 ml) salt. Add milk slowly and stir constantly until thick.

- Add mushrooms, mushroom soup, pimentos, diced chicken and chicken broth. Cook noodles according to package directions. Drain.

- Mix noodles with sauce and stir gently. Pour mixture into 10 x 15-inch (25 x 38 cm) baking dish. Sprinkle with cheese and cover and refrigerate until baking time.

- When ready to bake, preheat oven to 350° (175° C).

- Bake for 20 to 30 minutes until it heats thoroughly. Serves 12 to 14.

Happy Chicken Bake

**6 boneless, skinless chicken
    breast halves**
**1 (8 ounce) bottle Catalina
    dressing** **230 g**
**1 (1 ounce) packet onion
    soup mix** **30 g**
**1 (12 ounce) jar apricot
    preserves** **340 g**
1 tablespoon lime juice **15 ml**
Rice, cooked

• Preheat oven to 325° (160° C).

• Place chicken breasts in sprayed
  9 x 13-inch (23 x 33 cm)
  baking dish.

• Combine Catalina dressing, soup
  mix, apricot preserves and lime
  juice in saucepan. Heat just
  enough to mix.

• Pour over chicken breasts.
  Cover and bake for 1 hour
  10 minutes. Serve over rice.
  Serves 8.

Flaky Chicken

**8 boneless, skinless chicken
    breast halves**
¾ cup mayonnaise **170 g**
2 cups crushed corn flakes **55 g**
**½ cup grated parmesan
    cheese** **50 g**

• Preheat oven to 325° (160° C).

• Sprinkle chicken with a little
  salt and pepper. Dip chicken
  in mayonnaise and spread
  mayonnaise over chicken
  with brush.

• Combine corn flake crumbs and
  cheese in bowl and dip chicken
  in corn flake mixture until it
  completely coats chicken.

• Place chicken in sprayed
  9 x 13-inch (23 x 33 cm) glass
  baking dish and bake for 1 hour.
  Serves 8.

Fiesta Chicken

½ cup (1 stick) butter	115 g
2 cups finely crushed cheese crackers	120 g
1 (1 ounce) packet taco seasoning mix	30 g
5 - 6 boneless, skinless chicken breast halves, flattened	
1 bunch fresh green onions with tops, chopped	
1 teaspoon dry chicken bouillon granules	5 ml
1 (1 pint) carton whipping cream	500 ml
1 (8 ounce) package shredded Monterey Jack cheese	230 g
1 (4 ounce) can chopped green chilies	115 g

- Preheat oven to 350° (175° C).

- Melt butter in large baking dish and set aside. Combine cracker crumbs and taco mix in bowl. Dredge chicken in crumb mixture and pat mixture well to use all cracker crumbs.

- Place chicken breasts in sprayed 9 x 13-inch (23 x 33 cm) baking dish with melted butter. Take out several tablespoons melted butter and place in saucepan. Add onions and saute.

- Turn heat off, add chicken bouillon and stir. Add whipping cream, cheese, chopped green chilies and mix well. Pour over chicken in baking dish.

- Bake for 55 minutes. Serves 6.

Golden Chicken

6 boneless, skinless chicken
    breast halves
¼ cup (½ stick) butter   **60 g**
1 (10 ounce) can golden
    mushroom soup   **280 g**
½ cup sliced almonds   **95 g**

- Preheat oven to 350° (175° C).

- Place chicken breasts in sprayed
  9 x 13-inch (23 x 33 cm)
  baking pan.

- Combine butter, soup, almonds
  and ¼ cup (60 ml) water in
  saucepan. Heat and mix just
  until butter melts. Pour mixture
  over chicken.

- Cover and bake for 1 hour.
  Serves 6.

Four-Legged Chicken

4 boneless, skinless chicken
    breast halves
4 boneless, skinless, thighs
4 legs, skinned
¾ cup honey   **255 g**
½ cup mustard   **125 g**
½ cup (1 stick) butter,
    melted   **115 g**
1 teaspoon curry powder   **5 ml**
1 teaspoon minced cilantro   **5 ml**

- Preheat oven to 350° (175° C).

- Arrange all chicken pieces
  in sprayed 10 x 15-inch
  (25 x 38 cm) baking dish.
  Mix honey, mustard, butter,
  1 teaspoon (5 ml) salt, curry
  powder and cilantro in bowl.
  Spread evenly over chicken
  pieces.

- Bake for 30 minutes, remove
  from oven and baste chicken
  with pan juices. Return to
  oven and bake for an additional
  30 minutes or until chicken is
  golden brown. Serves 8.

Ginger Orange-Glazed Cornish Hens

1 cup fresh orange juice	250 ml
2 tablespoons plus ½ teaspoon peeled, minced fresh ginger	30 ml/2 ml
1 tablespoon soy sauce	15 ml
3 tablespoons honey	30 g
2 (1½ pounds) cornish hens, halved	2 (680 g)

- Preheat oven to 400° (205° C).

- Combine orange juice, 2 tablespoons (30 ml) minced ginger, soy sauce and honey in saucepan and cook on high heat, stirring constantly for 3 minutes or until thick and glossy.

- Place hens in sprayed 9x 13-inch (23 x 33 cm) baking pan and sprinkle ½ teaspoon (2 ml) ginger and ½ teaspoon (2 ml) each of salt and pepper over birds.

- Spoon glaze mixture over hens and bake for 25 minutes. Brush glaze over hens several times during cooking. Serves 2 to 4.

A Cornish game hen weighs about 2 pounds and is usually sold whole. This hen is best roasted or grilled.

Creamy Soup Chicken

6 - 8 boneless, skinless chicken
   breast halves
1 (10 ounce) can golden
   mushroom soup   280 g
1 cup white wine or white
   cooking wine   250 ml
1 (8 ounce) carton sour
   cream   230 g
Rice, cooked

- Preheat oven to 350° (175° C).

- Place chicken breasts in sprayed 9 x 13-inch (23 x 33 cm) baking pan, sprinkle with a little salt and pepper and bake for 30 minutes.

- Combine soup, wine and sour cream in saucepan and heat enough to mix well.

- Remove chicken from oven and cover with sour cream mixture.

- Reduce heat to 300° (150° C) and return to oven for an additional 30 minutes. Baste twice. Serve over rice. Serves 8.

Honey-Baked Chicken

2 whole chickens, quartered
½ cup (1 stick) butter,
    melted   **115 g**
⅔ cup honey   **95 g**
¼ cup dijon-style mustard   **60 g**
1 teaspoon curry powder   **5 ml**

- Preheat oven to 350° (175° C).

- Place chicken pieces skin-side up in large, shallow baking dish and sprinkle with a little salt.

- Combine butter, honey, mustard and curry powder in bowl and pour over chicken.

- Bake for 1 hour 5 minutes and baste every 20 minutes. Serves 8.

Honey-Mustard Chicken

⅓ cup dijon-style mustard   **85 g**
½ cup honey   **170 g**
2 tablespoons dried dill   **30 ml**
4 chicken quarters

- Preheat oven to 350° (175° C).

- Combine mustard, honey and dill in bowl. Arrange chicken quarters in sprayed 9 x 13-inch (23 x 33 cm) baking dish.

- Pour mustard mixture over chicken. Turn chicken over and make sure mustard mixture covers chicken.

- Cover and bake for 35 minutes. Uncover and bake for an additional 10 minutes. Serves 4 to 6.

Lemonade Chicken

6 boneless, skinless chicken
   breast halves
1 (6 ounce) can frozen
   lemonade concentrate,
   thawed   168 g
⅓ cup soy sauce   75 ml
1 teaspoon garlic powder   5 ml

- Preheat oven to 350° (175° C).

- Place chicken in sprayed 9 x 13-inch (23 x 33 cm) baking dish.

- Combine lemonade, soy sauce and garlic powder in bowl and pour over chicken.

- Cover and bake for 45 minutes. Uncover, pour juices over chicken and cook for an additional 10 minutes. Serves 4.

Oregano Chicken

¼ cup (½ stick) butter,
   melted   60 g
1 (.4 ounce) packet dry
   Italian salad
   dressing mix   10 g
2 tablespoons lemon juice 30 ml
4 boneless, skinless chicken
   breast halves
2 tablespoons dried oregano 30 ml

- Preheat oven to 350° (175° C).

- Combine butter, salad dressing mix and lemon juice in bowl. Place chicken in 9 x 13-inch (23 x 33 cm) baking pan and spoon butter mixture over chicken.

- Cover and bake for 45 minutes. Uncover, baste with pan drippings and sprinkle with oregano. Bake for an additional 15 minutes or until chicken juices run clear. Serves 4.

Herb-Roasted Turkey

Dry Rub:

2 tablespoons poultry seasoning	30 ml
2 teaspoons paprika	10 ml
2 teaspoons garlic powder	10 ml
½ teaspoon ground nutmeg	2 ml

Turkey:

1 (12 pound) turkey, thawed	5.4 kg
1 large onion, cut in wedges	
2 tablespoons oil	30 ml

- Preheat oven to 325° (175° C). '

- Combine all dry rub seasonings with 2 tablespoons (30 ml) salt and 1 teaspoon (5 ml) pepper in small bowl.

- Rinse turkey under cold water and pat dry. Place onion wedges in turkey cavity and rub about half of rub ingredients inside.

- Place turkey, breast-side up on shallow roasting pan lined with heavy foil. Spread oil over outside of turkey. Sprinkle remaining rub mixture over outside and add ½ cup (125 ml) water to roasting pan.

- Cover loosely with heavy foil and bake for about 3 hours 30 minutes or until meat thermometer inserted in breast reaches 175° (80° C). Let stand for about 15 minutes before carving. Reserve pan juices for gravy.

Turkey Gravy:

1 (1 ounce) packet turkey gravy mix	30 g
3 tablespoons flour	20 g
1 cup pan drippings or canned turkey broth	250 ml

- Combine gravy mix and flour in saucepan. Slowly stir in pan drippings and 1 cup (250 ml) water, stirring constantly.

- Bring to a boil, reduce heat and stir constantly until mixture thickens. Serves 16 to 20.

Home-Style Southwest Chicken

2 cups fine breadcrumbs	120 g
1 tablespoon cumin	15 ml
2 teaspoons chili powder	10 ml
½ teaspoon oregano	2 ml
4 eggs	
½ cup prepared green chile salsa	130 g
2 cloves garlic, minced	
3 tablespoons butter	35 g
3 - 4 pounds boneless, skinless chicken breast halves	1.4 – 1.8 kg
Iceberg lettuce	
Sour cream	
1 avocado	
1 lime	
Green onions with tops, chopped	

- Preheat oven to 350° (175° C).

- Combine breadcrumbs, cumin, chili powder, ½ teaspoon (2 ml) salt and oregano in large, shallow bowl and set aside. In separate bowl, beat eggs with salsa and garlic.

- Melt butter in 9 x 13-inch (23 x 33 cm) baking dish in oven. Dip chicken pieces into egg bowl and coat with breadcrumb mixture. Place pieces in baking dish and turn each piece in butter. Bake for about 35 to 40 minutes or until chicken is done.

- Place several leaves of iceberg lettuce on plate and serve chicken on top. Garnish with sour cream, avocado slices, lime slices and chopped green onion. Serves 4.

Lemon-Almond Chicken

Asparagus, lemon juice, curry powder and almonds give a flavorful twist to an otherwise ordinary chicken dish.

2 (15 ounce) cans cut asparagus, well drained	2 (425 g)
4 boneless, skinless chicken breast halves	
3 tablespoons butter	35 g
1 (10 ounce) can cream of asparagus soup	280 g
⅔ cup mayonnaise	150 g
¼ cup milk	60 ml
1 red bell pepper, cut in strips	
2 tablespoons lemon juice	30 ml
1 teaspoon curry powder	5 ml
¼ teaspoon ground ginger	1 ml
½ cup sliced almonds, toasted	95 g

- Preheat oven to 350° (175° C).

- Place asparagus in sprayed 7 x 11-inch (18 x 28 cm) baking dish and set aside. Sprinkle chicken with ½ teaspoon (2 ml) salt. Saute chicken in butter in large skillet for about 15 minutes and cut into strips.

- Spoon chicken over asparagus. Combine asparagus soup, mayonnaise, milk, bell pepper, lemon juice, curry powder, ginger and ¼ teaspoon (1 ml) pepper in skillet and heat just enough to mix well.

- Spoon over chicken and sprinkle almonds over top of casserole. Bake for 35 minutes. Serves 8 to 10.

Lemon-Herb Chicken

6 boneless, skinless chicken
   breast halves
1 cup (2 sticks) butter,
   melted, divided   230 g
1 cup flour   120 g

- Preheat oven to 350° (175° C).

- Dip each chicken breast in butter
  and flour and place in sprayed
  9 x 13-inch

- (23 x 33 cm) baking dish. Cover
  and bake for 30 minutes.

Lemon-Herb Sauce:

¼ cup lemon juice	60 ml
½ teaspoon lemon pepper	2 ml
½ teaspoon garlic powder	2 ml
2 tablespoons brown sugar	30 g
½ teaspoon oregano	2 ml
½ teaspoon crushed	
rosemary	2 ml
1 teaspoon lemon peel	5 ml
White rice, cooked	

- While chicken is cooking, add
  Lemon-Herb Sauce ingredients
  to mixing bowl with remaining
  butter, ½ teaspoon (2 ml) salt
  and ¼ cup (60 ml) hot water and
  mix well.

- After chicken cooks for
  30 minutes, uncover and
  pour Lemon-Herb Sauce over
  chicken. Bake for an additional
  25 minutes and serve over white
  rice. Serves 5.

Montezuma Celebration Chicken

6 boneless, skinless chicken
**   breast halves**
1 green bell pepper, seeded,
**   cut in rings**
1 (16 ounce) jar hot salsa   455 g
⅔ cup packed brown sugar   150 g
1 tablespoon mustard   15 ml

- Preheat oven to 350° (175° C).

- Place chicken breasts covered with bell pepper rings in sprayed 9 x 13-inch (23 x 33 cm) baking dish without breasts touching each other. Combine salsa, brown sugar, mustard and ½ teaspoon (2 ml) salt in bowl and spoon over each piece of chicken.

- Cover and bake for 35 to 40 minutes. Uncover and continue cooking for additional 10 to 15 minutes to let chicken breasts brown slightly. Serves 6.

A pip is the first small holes pecked through the eggshell as a chick gets ready to hatch.

Celebration Chicken

6 boneless, skinless chicken
    breast halves
1 green bell pepper, seeded,
    cut in rings
1 (16 ounce) jar hot salsa   **455 g**
⅔ cup packed brown sugar   **150 g**
1 tablespoon mustard   **15 ml**

- Preheat oven to 350° (175° C).

- Place chicken breasts covered with bell pepper rings in sprayed 9 x 13-inch

- (23 x 33 cm) baking dish without breasts touching each other. Combine salsa, brown sugar, mustard and ½ teaspoon (2 ml) salt in bowl and spoon over each piece of chicken.

- Cover and bake for 35 to 40 minutes. Uncover and continue cooking for additional 10 to 15 minutes to let chicken breasts brown slightly.

Mozzarella Chicken

4 boneless, skinless chicken
    breast halves
1 cup dry Italian-seasoned
    breadcrumbs   **120 g**
1 cup prepared spaghetti
    sauce   **250 g**
4 slices mozzarella cheese

- Preheat oven to 350° (175° C).

- Pound each chicken breast to flatten slightly. Coat chicken well in breadcrumbs and arrange in sprayed 9 x 13-inch (23 x 33 cm) baking dish.

- Spread quarter of sauce over each portion. Place 1 slice cheese over each and garnish with remaining breadcrumbs. Bake for 45 minutes. Serves 4.

Nacho Chicken

1 chicken, quartered
2 (10 ounce) cans fiesta
    nacho cheese soup   **2 (280 g)**
¾ cup milk   **175 ml**
3 tablespoons white
    wine Worcestershire
    sauce   **45 ml**

- Preheat oven to 350° (175° C).

- Place chicken quarters in sprayed 9 x 13-inch (23 x 33 cm) baking pan with sides.

- Combine soup, milk and Worcestershire in saucepan and heat just enough to mix well. Spread over chicken.

- Cover and bake for 1 hour. Serves 8 to 10.

One-Dish Chicken Bake

1 (1 ounce) packet vegetable
    soup mix   **30 g**
1 (6 ounce) package chicken
    stuffing mix   **170 g**
4 boneless, skinless chicken
    breast halves
1 (10 ounce) can cream of
    mushroom soup   **280 g**
⅓ cup sour cream   **80 g**

- Preheat oven to 375° (190° C).

- Toss contents of vegetable soup mix, stuffing mix and 1⅔ cups (400 ml) water in bowl and set aside.

- Place chicken in sprayed 9 x 13-inch (23 x 33 cm) baking dish.

- Mix soup and sour cream in saucepan over low heat just enough to pour over chicken. Spoon stuffing evenly over top.

- Bake for 40 minutes. Serves 4.

Onion-Sweet Chicken

2 chickens, quartered
1 (16 ounce) can whole
    cranberry sauce 455 g
1 (8 ounce) bottle Catalina
    salad dressing 250 ml
1 (1 ounce) packet onion
    soup mix 30 g

- Preheat oven to 350° (175° C).

- Place chicken quarters in sprayed 10 x 15-inch (25 x 38 cm) baking dish. Combine cranberry sauce, salad dressing and soup mix in bowl, blend well and pour over chicken.

- Cover and bake for 1 hour 10 minutes. Before last 10 minutes, uncover chicken and place back in oven to brown. Serves 6 to 8.

TIP: Remove wings from chicken breasts, if you like.

Oven-Glazed Chicken

4 boneless, skinless chicken
    breast halves
1 (10 ounce) can Italian
    tomato soup 280 g
2 tablespoons white wine
    Worcestershire sauce 30 ml
2 tablespoons packed brown
    sugar 30 g

- Preheat oven to 350° (175° C).

- Place chicken breasts in sprayed 7 x 11-inch (18 x 28 cm) baking dish.

- Combine tomato soup, Worcestershire sauce and brown sugar in small bowl and mix well. Spoon over chicken.

- Bake for 1 hour. Serves 4.

Oven-Fried Ranch Chicken

1 medium chicken, cut into
   serving pieces
1 (.4 ounce) packet ranch
   buttermilk salad
   dressing mix   **10 g**
1 cup buttermilk*   **250 ml**
½ cup mayonnaise   **110 g**
2 - 3 cups crushed corn
   flakes   **55 - 85 g**

- Preheat oven to 350° (175° C).

- Pat chicken pieces dry and place on paper towels.

- Combine ranch dressing mix, buttermilk and mayonnaise in shallow bowl and mix well.

- Dip chicken pieces in dressing and cover well. Roll each piece in corn flakes and coat all sides well.

- Arrange pieces so they do not touch in sprayed 9 x 13-inch (23 x 33 cm) baking dish. Bake for 1 hour. Serves 8.

TIP: *To make buttermilk, mix 1 cup (250 ml) milk with 1 tablespoon (15 ml) lemon juice or vinegar and let milk sit about 10 minutes.*

Q: Why did the chicken cross the road halfway?

A: She wanted to lay it on the line.

Oven-Herb Chicken

2 cups crushed corn flakes	55 g
½ cup grated parmesan cheese	50 g
1 tablespoon rosemary	15 ml
1 tablespoon thyme leaves	15 ml
1 teaspoon oregano	5 ml
1 tablespoon parsley flakes	15 ml
½ teaspoon garlic powder	2 ml
½ cup (1 stick) butter, melted	115 g
5 - 6 boneless, skinless chicken breast halves or 1 chicken, quartered	

- Preheat oven to 325° (160° C).

- Combine corn flakes, parmesan cheese, rosemary, thyme, oregano, parsley, garlic powder, ½ teaspoon (2 ml) salt and 1 teaspoon (5 ml) pepper in medium bowl.

- In separate bowl, melt butter in microwave. Dip chicken breasts in butter and corn flake mixture; coat well.

- Place chicken in sprayed 9 x 13-inch (23 x 33 cm) shallow baking dish. (Do not crowd pieces.) Bake for 1 hour. Serve 8.

Oven-Fried Chicken

⅔ cup fine dry
    breadcrumbs   40 g
⅓ cup grated parmesan
    cheese   35 g
½ teaspoon garlic salt   2 ml
½ cup Italian salad
    dressing   125 ml
6 boneless, skinless chicken
    breast halves

- Preheat oven to 350° (175° C).

- Combine breadcrumbs, cheese and garlic salt in shallow bowl.

- In separate shallow bowl, place salad dressing. Dip chicken in salad dressing and dredge in crumb mixture.

- Place chicken in 9 x 13-inch (23 x 33 cm) sprayed baking pan.

- Bake for 50 minutes. Serves 6.

Oven-Fried Turkey

1 - 1½ pounds turkey
    tenderloins,
    thawed   455 - 680 g
1 (5.5 ounce) package
    baked chicken
    coating mix   155 g

- Preheat oven to 400° (205° C).

- Place all tenderloin strips on several pieces of paper towels to partially dry.

- Pour chicken coating mix into shallow bowl and press both sides of each piece of turkey into seasoned coating.

- Place in sprayed 9 x 13-inch (23 x 33 cm) baking pan so pieces do not touch. Bake for 20 to 30 minutes or until turkey is light brown. Serves 12.

Parmesan-Crusted Chicken

1 egg white, beaten	
1½ cups dry breadcrumbs	180 g
1 teaspoon dried parsley	5 ml
½ cup grated parmesan cheese	50 g
4 small boneless, skinless chicken breast halves	
Olive oil	

- Preheat oven to 425° (220° C).

- Combine beaten egg white and 1 tablespoon (15 ml) water in bowl.

- In separate bowl, combine breadcrumbs, parsley, cheese and a little salt and pepper.

- Dip each piece of chicken in egg white and dredge in crumb mixture. Place in heavy skillet with a little oil and saute chicken until golden on both sides, about 5 minutes.

- Transfer to sprayed 7 x 11-inch (18 x 28 cm) baking dish and bake for 15 minutes.

Sage-Butter Sauce:

¼ cup minced shallots	60 ml
Olive oil	
½ cup dry white wine	125 ml
½ cup whipping cream	125 ml
½ cup chicken broth	125 ml
¼ cup (½ stick) butter, cubed	60 g
¾ teaspoon dried sage	4 ml

- Saute shallots in a little oil in saucepan.

- Add wine, cream and chicken broth. Simmer until it reduces by half. Stir in butter and sage. Serve over parmesan chicken. Serves 4.

Party Chicken Breasts

6 boneless, skinless chicken
    breast halves
6 strips bacon
1 (2.5 ounce) jar dried beef   70 g
1 (10 ounce) can cream of
    chicken soup   280 g
1 (8 ounce) carton sour
    cream   230 g

- Preheat oven to 325° (160° C).

- Wrap each chicken breast with 1 strip bacon and secure with toothpicks.

- Place dried beef in bottom of sprayed 9 x 13-inch (23 x 33 cm) baking pan and top with chicken.

- Heat soup and sour cream in saucepan, just enough to pour over chicken.

- Bake for 1 hour. Serves 6 to 8.

Peachy Chicken

½ cup Italian dressing   125 ml
2 teaspoons ground ginger   10 ml
4 boneless, skinless chicken
    breast halves
⅓ cup peach preserves   110 g

- Combine Italian dressing and ginger in large resealable plastic bag. Place chicken in plastic bag and turn several times to coat chicken.

- Marinate in refrigerator, turning occasionally for 4 hours or overnight. When ready to cook, remove chicken and discard marinade. Save ⅓ cup (75 ml) marinade.

- Bring saved marinade in small saucepan to a boil for 1 minute. Remove from heat, stir in peach preserves and set aside.

- Broil chicken until juices run clear and brush with mixture last 5 minutes of cooking. Serves 4.

Picante Chicken

4 boneless, skinless chicken
    breast halves
1 (16 ounce) jar salsa   **455 g**
4 tablespoons brown sugar   **55 g**
1 tablespoon mustard   **15 ml**
Rice, cooked

- Preheat oven to 375° (190° C).

- Place chicken in shallow sprayed baking dish.

- Combine salsa, brown sugar and mustard in small bowl and pour over chicken.

- Bake for 45 minutes or until chicken juices run clear and serve over rice. Serves 4.

Rosemary Chicken

½ cup flour   **60 g**
1 tablespoon dried
    rosemary, divided   **15 ml**
½ cup Italian salad dressing   **125 ml**
4 - 5 boneless, skinless
    chicken breast halves

- Preheat oven to 350° (175° C).

- Combine flour and half rosemary in bowl.

- Pour a little Italian dressing in shallow bowl and dip chicken breasts in dressing.

- Dredge chicken in flour mixture. Place in sprayed 9 x 13-inch (23 x 33 cm) baking dish.

- Bake for 40 minutes. Remove from oven and sprinkle remaining rosemary over breasts and cook for an additional 10 minutes. Serves 4.

Pimento Cheese-Stuffed Fried Chicken

4 boneless, skinless chicken
   breast halves
½ cup milk   **125 ml**
1 large egg, beaten
2 cups seasoned
   breadcrumbs   **240 g**
Olive oil
1 (16 ounce) carton
   pimento cheese   **455 g**

- Preheat oven to 350° (175° C).

- Dry chicken breasts with paper towels and sprinkle well with a little salt and pepper.

- Combine milk and beaten egg in shallow bowl and mix well. In separate shallow bowl, place breadcrumbs.

- Dip chicken in milk mixture and dredge in breadcrumbs.

- Pour oil to ⅛-inch (3 mm) depth and cook chicken in large skillet over medium-high heat for about 10 to 12 minutes on each side. Transfer to sprayed 9 x 13-inch (23 x 33 cm) baking sheet.

- Hold chicken with tongs and cut slit in 1 side of each chicken breast to form pocket. Spoon about ¼ cup (55 g) pimento cheese into each pocket and bake for about 3 minutes or until cheese melts. Serves 4.

Pimento-Chicken Enchilada Bake

10 corn tortillas
1 (10 ounce) can cream
of mushroom soup   **280 g**
1 (10 ounce) can cream
of chicken soup   **280 g**
1 cup milk   **250 ml**
1 small onion, chopped
2 (4 ounce) cans diced,
green chilies   **2 (115 g)**
2 (4 ounce) jars diced
pimentos, drained   **2 (115 g)**
5 boneless, skinless
chicken breast halves,
cooked
1 (12 ounce) package
shredded cheddar
cheese   **340 g**

- Preheat oven to 350° (175° C).

- Cut tortillas into 1-inch (2.5 cm) strips and lay half of them in sprayed baking dish. Mix mushroom soup, chicken soup, milk, onion, green chilies and pimentos in saucepan and heat just enough to mix.

- Chop cooked chicken and place half on top of tortilla strips. Pour half of sauce on top of chicken, repeat tortilla layer and sauce layer. Cover and bake for 45 minutes. Sprinkle cheese over casserole, return to oven and bake for an additional 5 minutes. Serves 5.

TIP: If you want to make this dish in advance, top with cheese and refrigerate overnight. Bake the next day when you need it.

Pop's Pleasing Pasta

1 (14 ounce) package frozen, cooked, breaded chicken cutlets, thawed	400 g
1 (28 ounce) jar spaghetti sauce, divided	795 g
2 (5 ounce) packages grated parmesan cheese, divided	2 (145 g)
1 (8 ounce) package thin spaghetti, cooked	230 g

- Preheat oven to 400° (205° C).

- Place cutlets and top each with about ¼ cup (65 g) spaghetti sauce and heaping tablespoon (15 ml) parmesan in sprayed 9 x 13-inch (23 x 33 cm) baking dish. Bake for 15 minutes.

- Place cooked spaghetti on serving platter and top with cutlets.

- Sprinkle remaining cheese over cutlets. Heat remaining spaghetti sauce and serve with chicken and spaghetti. Serves 6.

The longest recorded flight of a chicken is 13 seconds.

Prairie Spring Chicken

2 pounds chicken thighs	910 g
Olive oil	
¾ cup chili sauce	205 g
¾ cup packed brown sugar	165 g
1 (1 ounce) packet onion soup mix	30 g
⅛ teaspoon cayenne pepper	.5 ml
Rice, cooked	

- Preheat oven to 325° (160° C).

- Brown chicken in skillet with oil and place in sprayed 9 x 13-inch (23 x 33 cm) baking dish.

- Combine chili sauce, brown sugar, dry soup mix, cayenne pepper and ½ cup (125 ml) water in bowl and pour over chicken.

- Cover and bake for 20 minutes. Uncover and bake for an additional 15 minutes. Serve over rice. Serves 8.

Ranch Chicken

½ cup parmesan cheese	50 g
1½ cups corn flakes	40 g
1 (.4 ounce) packet ranch-style salad dressing mix	10 g
2 pounds chicken drumsticks	910 g
½ cup (1 stick) butter, melted	115 g

- Preheat oven to 350° (175° C).

- Combine cheese, corn flakes and dressing mix in bowl.

- Dip washed, dried chicken in melted butter and dredge in corn flake mixture.

- Bake for 50 minutes or until golden brown. Serves 8.

Reuben Chicken

4 boneless, skinless chicken
  breast halves
4 slices Swiss cheese
1 (15 ounce) can sauerkraut,
  drained   425 g
1 (8 ounce) bottle Catalina
  salad dressing   250 ml

- Preheat oven to 350° (175° C).

- Arrange chicken breasts in
  sprayed 7 x 11-inch
  (18 x 28 cm) baking pan.

- Place cheese over chicken and
  spread sauerkraut next. Cover
  with dressing.

- Bake covered for 30 minutes.
  Uncover and cook for an
  additional 15 minutes. Serves 4.

Ritzy Chicken

6 boneless, skinless
  chicken breast
  halves
1 (8 ounce) carton sour
  cream   230 g
⅓ (12 ounce) box round
  buttery crackers,
  crushed   ⅓ (340 g)

- Preheat oven to 350° (175° C).

- Dip chicken in sour cream and
  roll in cracker crumbs with
  ¼ teaspoon (1 ml) pepper. Place
  chicken in sprayed 9 x 13-inch
  (23 x 33 cm) baking dish.

- Bake for 55 minutes. Serves 6.

Roasted Chicken

1 (3 - 4 pound) chicken   1.4 - 1.8 kg
3 tablespoons butter,
   softened   35 g

- Preheat oven to 350° (175° C).

- Wash and dry chicken with paper towels. Remove giblet package from cavity. Spread butter over breasts, legs and wings. Salt and pepper liberally.

- Place chicken on back in deep roasting pan. Bake for 20 to 30 minutes per pound or until juices run clear.

- Baste frequently, add water if necessary. Turn bird occasionally to brown evenly. Serves 8.

TIP: *Basting with pan juices will make a glazed coating on chicken. For a crusted topping on chicken, sprinkle flour over bird after spreading butter on outside.*

Roasted Chicken Supreme

This is such an easy recipe and good for any meal.

1 (3 pound) whole chicken   1.4 kg
1 rib celery
1 onion
Canola oil
Paprika

- Preheat oven to 325° (160° C).

- Wash chicken and dry with paper towels. Cut celery in half. Insert celery and onion into chicken cavity. Tie legs together, rub chicken with oil and sprinkle with paprika.

- Roast in open pan for 20 to 30 minutes per pound of chicken or until juices run clear. Baste every 40 minutes. To serve, remove onion and celery. (You can save and reuse for soup or stew.) Chicken will be extra juicy and moist with no onion flavor. Serves 6.

Roasted Chicken and Vegetables

2 pounds boneless chicken breasts	**910 g**
1 cup lemon pepper marinade with lemon juice, divided	**250 ml**
1 (16 ounce) package frozen mixed vegetables, thawed	**455 g**
¼ cup olive oil	**60 ml**

- Preheat oven to 375° (190° C).

- Arrange chicken skin-side down in sprayed 9 x 13-inch (23 x 33 cm) baking pan. Pour ⅔ cup (150 ml) marinade over chicken. Bake for 30 minutes.

- Turn chicken over and baste with remaining ⅓ cup (75 ml) marinade.

- Toss vegetables with olive oil and 1 tablespoon (15 ml) salt. Arrange vegetables around chicken and cover with foil. Return pan to oven and bake for an additional 20 to 30 minutes or until juices run clear. Serves 8 to 10.

In Gainesville, Georgia – the chicken capital of the world – it's illegal to eat chicken with a fork.

Pineapple-Teriyaki Chicken

**6 boneless, skinless chicken
    breast halves**
½ red onion, sliced
**1 green bell pepper, seeded,
    sliced**
1 cup teriyaki marinade   240 ml
**1 (15 ounce) can pineapple
    rings with juice   425 g**

- Preheat oven to 350° (175° C).

- Place chicken in sprayed
  9 x 13-inch (23 x 33 cm) baking
  dish and arrange vegetables
  over chicken.

- Mix teriyaki with juice from
  pineapple. Pour over vegetables
  and chicken.

- Bake for 45 minutes. Spoon
  juices over chicken once
  during baking.

- About 10 minutes before
  chicken is done, place pineapple
  slices over chicken and return to
  oven. Serves 6.

Saucy Chicken

**5 - 6 boneless, skinless
    chicken breast halves**
**1 (16 ounce) jar
    thick-and-chunky salsa   455 g**
**1 cup packed light brown
    sugar   220 g**
**1½ tablespoons dijon-style
    mustard   25 g**
Rice, cooked

* Preheat oven to 350° (175° C).

* Place chicken breasts in sprayed
  9 x 13-inch (23 x 33 cm)
  baking dish.

* Combine salsa, sugar and
  mustard in bowl and pour
  over chicken.

* Cover and bake for 45 minutes.
  Serve over rice. Serves 6.

Sunday Chicken

**5 - 6 boneless, skinless
    chicken breast halves**
½ cup sour cream   120 g
¼ cup soy sauce   60 ml
**1 (10 ounce) can French
    onion soup   280 g**

* Preheat oven to 350° (175° C).

* Place chicken in sprayed
  9 x 13-inch (23 x 33 cm)
  baking dish.

* Combine sour cream, soy sauce
  and soup in saucepan and heat
  just enough to mix well. Pour
  over chicken breasts.

* Cover and bake for 55 minutes.
  Serves 6.

Saucy Chicken Breasts

This sauce really makes a delicious chicken dish!

1½ cups mayonnaise	335 g
½ cup cider vinegar	125 ml
¼ cup lemon juice	60 ml
⅓ cup sugar	70 g
3 tablespoons white wine Worcestershire sauce*	45 ml
5 boneless, skinless chicken breast halves	

- Combine mayonnaise, vinegar, lemon juice, sugar and white Worcestershire sauce in saucepan and mix well with whisk until mixture is smooth.

- Pour half mixture into resealable plastic bag with chicken breasts and marinate for 4 to 6 hours. Move chicken around a couple of times to make sure marinade covers chicken.

- When ready to cook, preheat oven to 350° (175° C). Place chicken breasts in sprayed 9 x 13-inch (23 x 33 cm) baking pan (so each breast does not touch). Pour remaining half of marinade from bag over chicken. Sprinkle pepper generously over breasts.

- Cook for 50 to 60 minutes. If chicken breasts are not slightly brown, place under broiler for 3 to 4 minutes, but watch closely.

- Do not let sauce between chicken breasts get brown. It is done when sauce is just light brown or until juices run clear. Serves 6.

TIP: White wine Worcestershire sauce will give you a pleasing color and flavor.

Savory Oven-Fried Chicken

2 cups crushed corn flakes	55 g
½ cup grated parmesan cheese	50 g
1 tablespoon rosemary	15 ml
1 tablespoon thyme leaves	15 ml
1 teaspoon oregano	5 ml
1 tablespoon parsley flakes	15 ml
½ teaspoon garlic powder	2 ml
½ cup (1 stick) butter, melted	115 g
8 boneless, skinless chicken breast halves	

- Preheat oven to 325° (160° C).

- Mix corn flakes, parmesan cheese, rosemary, thyme, oregano, parsley, garlic powder, ½ teaspoon (2 ml) salt and 1 teaspoon (5 ml) pepper in medium bowl.

- In separate bowl, place melted butter. Dip chicken in butter and corn flake mixture.

- Place in sprayed 9 x 13-inch (23 x 33 cm) baking dish. Do not crowd pieces. Bake for 1 hour. Serves 8.

Springy Chicken

4 - 5 boneless, skinless
   chicken breast halves
1 tablespoon oregano   15 ml
¾ teaspoon garlic powder   4 ml
½ cup (1 stick) butter,
   melted   115 g

- Place chicken breasts in resealable plastic bag and add oregano and garlic powder. Marinate in refrigerator for 3 or 4 hours.

- When ready to bake, preheat oven to 325° (160° C).

- Place chicken and butter in sprayed 9 x 13-inch (23 x 33 cm) baking dish. Cover and bake for 1 hour. Serves 5.

Real Simple Cornish Game Hens

4 (2 pound) Cornish
   game hens   4 (910 g)
Canola oil
2 teaspoons paprika   10 ml
Fresh cracked black
   pepper

- Preheat oven to 350° (175°C).

- Wash and dry hens and place in sprayed baking pan. Rub outside with oil. Sprinkle paprika, lots of black pepper and a little salt over each.

- Bake for 1 hour 30 minutes to 2 hours or until juices run clear. Serves 4.

Sesame Chicken

½ **cup flour**	**60 g**
½ **teaspoon chili powder**	**2 ml**
¼ **teaspoon paprika**	**1 ml**
½ **teaspoon onion salt**	**2 ml**
½ **teaspoon celery salt**	**2 ml**
1 **teaspoon lemon pepper**	**5 ml**
1 **teaspoon garlic powder**	**5 ml**
8 **boneless, skinless chicken breast halves**	
½ **cup (1 stick) butter, melted**	**115 g**
1 **cup sesame seeds, lightly toasted**	**130 g**

- Preheat oven to 350° (175° C).

- Thoroughly mix flour, chili powder, paprika, onion salt, celery salt, lemon pepper and garlic powder in bowl.

- Roll chicken breasts in flour mixture and continue to roll chicken until all flour mixture is used.

- Dip floured chicken in butter and roll in sesame seeds. Place chicken breasts in sprayed 10 x 15-inch (25 x 38 cm) baking dish. Pour any extra butter in baking dish and bake for 1 hour. Serves 8.

Q: What is a haunted chicken?

A: A poultry-geist.

Soft Chicken-Taco Bake

6 boneless, skinless chicken
    breast halves
1 (1 ounce) packet taco
    seasoning   30 g
1 (15 ounce) can kidney
    beans, rinsed, drained   425 g
1 large onion, chopped,
    divided
12 corn tortillas
1 cup half-and-half cream   250 ml
3 large tomatoes, chopped
1 tablespoon minced
    cilantro   15 ml
1 (12 ounce) package
    shredded cheddar
    cheese   340 g
1 (5 ounce) package Fiesta
    Sides Spanish rice   145 g

- Preheat oven to 325° (160° C).

- Boil chicken in just enough water to cover. When chicken cooks and is tender, season with taco seasoning and 1 tablespoon (15 ml) salt. Cool and chop or shred chicken.

- Place several tablespoons meat, several tablespoons beans and 1 teaspoon (5 ml) onion in middle of each tortilla. Roll and place side by side in sprayed 9 x 13-inch (23 x 33 cm) baking dish. Pour half-and-half cream over rolled tortillas.

- Combine tomatoes, remaining onion and cilantro and sprinkle evenly over rolled tortillas. Spread cheese over top of tomatoes and bake for 20 minutes or until cheese melts. Serve hot with Spanish rice. Serves 6.

Chicken-on-the-Border

**8 boneless, skinless chicken
    breast halves**
**1 cup shredded Monterey
    Jack cheese**   **240 ml**
**½ cup shredded cheddar
    cheese**   **120 ml**
**1 (4 ounce) can chopped
    green chilies, drained**   **115 g**
1 teaspoon cilantro   **5 ml**
3 tablespoons onion flakes   **45 ml**
⅓ cup (⅔ stick) butter   **80 ml**
2 teaspoons ground cumin   **10 ml**
1 teaspoon chili powder   **5 ml**
1 cup crushed tortilla chips

- Preheat oven to 350° (175° C).

- Pound chicken breasts to about ¼-inch (6 mm) thick. Mix cheeses, chilies, cilantro and onion in bowl.

- Place 2 to 3 tablespoons (15 to 20 g) cheese mixture on each chicken breast and roll and place seam-side down in sprayed 9 x 13-inch (23 x 33 cm) baking dish. Melt butter in saucepan, add cumin and chili powder and pour over chicken.

- Cover and bake for 30 minutes, uncover and top with crushed chips. Return to oven and bake for an additional 15 minutes. Serves 8.

Southern-Stuffed Peppers

6 large green peppers
½ pound chicken livers,
    chopped   **230 g**
6 slices bacon, diced
1 cup chopped onion   **160 g**
1 cup sliced celery   **100 g**
1 clove garlic, crushed
1 (4 ounce) can sliced
    mushrooms   **115 g**
2 cups cooked rice   **330 g**

- Preheat oven to 375° (190° C).

- Wash peppers, cut slice through stem end and remove seeds. Cook peppers about 5 minutes in small amount of boiling, salted water. Remove from water and drain.

- Cook chicken livers, bacon, onion, celery, garlic and 1 teaspoon (5 ml) salt in medium saucepan until vegetables are tender. Add mushrooms and rice; mix well. Stuff peppers with mixture.

- Arrange in sprayed baking pan, seal and freeze. To serve, thaw and add ½-inch (1.2 cm) water to pan, cover and bake for 20 to 25 minutes. Serves 6.

Spiced Spanish Chicken

2 cups instant rice	190 g
4 boneless, skinless, cooked chicken breast halves, cut into strips	
1 (15 ounce) can Mexican stewed tomatoes with liquid	425 g
1 (8 ounce) can tomato sauce	230 g
1 (15 ounce) can whole kernel corn, drained	425 g
1 (4 ounce) jar diced pimentos, drained	115 g
1 teaspoon chili powder	5 ml
1 teaspoon ground cumin	5 ml

- Preheat oven to 350° (175° C).

- Spread rice evenly in sprayed 3-quart (3 L) baking dish. Place chicken strips over top of rice.

- Combine stewed tomatoes, tomato sauce, corn, pimentos, chili powder, cumin and ½ teaspoon (2 ml) each of salt and pepper in large bowl and mix well.

- Slowly and easily pour mixture over chicken and rice. Cover and bake for 1 hour. Serves 6.

Southwest-Mexican Pizzas

Butter
6 (8 inch) flour tortillas   **6 (20 cm)**
1 (14 ounce) jar
    Mexican roasted
    ranchero sauce   **400 g**
1½ cups cooked,
    shredded chicken   **210 g**
1 poblano chile, roasted,
    peeled, chopped
4 fresh green onions,
    finely diced
1 (8 ounce) package
    shredded Monterey
    Jack cheese   **230 g**

- Preheat oven to 425° (220° C).

- Butter 1 side of tortilla and place tortillas, butter-side up on baking sheets. Bake for 4 to 5 minutes, just enough to crisp tortillas.

- Spread each tortilla with about ¼ to ⅓ cup (70 to 90 g) ranchero sauce, shredded chicken, chile pepper and green onions. Top with shredded cheese.

- Return to oven and bake just until cheese melts. Cut into wedges to serve. Serve 6.

TIP: *If you don't want to roast the poblano chile, just use a bell pepper.*

Spicy Chicken and Rice

3 cups cooked, sliced chicken	420 g
2 cups cooked brown rice	390 g
1 (10 ounce) can fiesta nacho cheese soup	280 g
1 (10 ounce) can chopped tomatoes and green chilies	280 g

- Preheat oven to 350° (175° C).

- Combine chicken, rice, cheese soup, tomatoes and green chilies in bowl and mix well.

- Spoon mixture into sprayed 3-quart (3 L) baking dish.

- Cover and bake for 45 minutes. Serves 5.

Sunshine Chicken

1 chicken, quartered	
Flour	
1 cup barbecue sauce	270 g
½ cup orange juice	125 ml

- Preheat oven to 350° (175° C).

- Place chicken in bowl of flour and coat well.

- Brown chicken in skillet and place in sprayed 9 x 13-inch (23 x 33 cm) baking pan.

- Combine barbecue sauce and orange juice in bowl. Pour over chicken.

- Cover and bake for 45 minutes. Remove from oven, spoon sauce over chicken and bake uncovered for an additional 20 minutes. Serves 4.

Succulent Pecan-Chicken Breasts

⅓ cup (⅔ stick) butter	75 g
1 cup flour	120 g
1 cup finely ground pecans	110 g
¼ cup sesame seeds	30 g
1 tablespoon paprika	15 ml
1 egg, beaten	
1 cup buttermilk*	250 ml
6 boneless, skinless chicken breast halves	
⅓ cup coarsely chopped pecans	40 g
Fresh parsley	

- Preheat oven to 350° (175° C).

- Melt butter in large 9 x 13-inch (23 x 33 cm) baking dish and set aside. Combine flour, finely ground pecans, sesame seeds, paprika, 1 teaspoon (5 ml) salt and ¼ teaspoon (1 ml) pepper in bowl.

- In separate bowl, combine egg and buttermilk. Dip chicken in egg mixture, dredge in flour mixture and coat well.

- Place chicken in baking dish and turn once to coat with butter. Sprinkle with chopped pecans and bake for 40 minutes or until golden brown. Garnish with fresh parsley. Serves 6 to 8.

TIP: *Chicken may be cut into strips, prepared the same way and used as an appetizer. A honey-mustard dressing would be nice for dipping. This recipe could also be used for fish, like orange roughy, if cooking time is reduced to half.*

*TIP: *To make buttermilk, mix 1 cup (250 ml) milk with 1 tablespoon (15 ml) lemon juice or vinegar and let milk rest for about 10 minutes.*

Sweet-and-Sour Chicken

6 boneless, skinless chicken
   breast halves
Olive oil
1 (1 ounce) packet onion
   soup mix   30 g
1 (6 ounce) can frozen
   orange juice
   concentrate, thawed   170 g

- Preheat oven to 350° (175° C).

- Brown chicken in a little oil or butter and place chicken in sprayed 9 x 13-inch (23 x 33 cm) baking dish.

- Combine onion soup mix, orange juice and ⅔ cup (150 ml) water in small bowl. Mix well and pour over chicken.

- Bake for 45 to 50 minutes. Serves 6.

Super Cheese Chicken

1 (10 ounce) can cream of
   chicken soup   280 g
1 cup regular brown rice   185 g
4 - 6 boneless, skinless
   chicken breast halves
1 (8 ounce) package
   shredded colby-Jack
   cheese   230 g

- Preheat oven to 350° (175° C).

- Combine soup, rice, 1½ cups (375 ml) water and a little salt and pepper in bowl.

- Place in 9 x 13-inch (23 x 33 cm) baking dish.

- Sprinkle chicken with additional pepper and place in baking dish with rice-soup mixture.

- Cover and bake for 50 minutes. Uncover, sprinkle cheese over chicken and serve. Serves 6.

Tangy Chicken

1 (2 pound) broiler-fryer chicken, cut up	910 g
3 tablespoons butter	35 g
½ cup steak sauce	135 g

- Preheat oven to 350° (175° C).

- Brown chicken pieces in skillet with butter and place in sprayed 9 x 13-inch (23 x 33cm) baking pan.

- Combine sauce and ½ cup (125 ml) water and pour over chicken.

- Cover and bake for 45 minutes. Uncover last 10 minutes of cooking time for chicken to brown. Chicken is done when juices run clear. Serves 6.

Tasty Turkey Crunch

1 (8 ounce) package noodles	230 g
2½ cups cooked, diced turkey	350 g
1 (1 ounce) packet chicken gravy, prepared	280 g
2 cups round, buttery cracker crumbs	120 g

- Preheat oven to 350° (175° C).

- Boil noodles according to package directions and drain.

- Arrange alternating layers of noodles, turkey and gravy in sprayed 2-quart (2 L) baking dish and cover with cracker crumbs.

- Bake for 35 minutes. Serves 6.

Turkey Burgers

2 pounds ground turkey   910 g
1 (16 ounce) jar hot
**   chipotle salsa, divided   455 g**
8 slices Monterey Jack cheese
Sesame seed hamburger buns

• Combine ground turkey with
  1 cup (265 g) salsa in large
  bowl. Mix well and shape into
  8 patties.

• Place patties on broiler pan and
  broil for 12 to 15 minutes. Turn
  once during cooking. Top each
  patty with cheese slice and grill
  just long enough to melt cheese.

• Place burgers on buns, spoon
  heaping tablespoon (15 ml)
  salsa over cheese and top with
  remaining half of bun. Serves 8.

Winey Chicken

6 boneless, skinless chicken
**   breast halves**
Olive oil
1 (10 ounce) can cream of
**   mushroom soup   280 g**
1 (10 ounce) can cream of
**   onion soup   280 g**
1 cup white wine   250 ml
Rice, cooked

• Preheat oven to 325° (160° C).

• Brown chicken in skillet with
  little bit of oil. Place in
  9 x 13-inch (23 x 33 cm)
  baking dish.

• Combine soups and wine and
  pour over chicken.

• Cover and bake for 35 minutes.
  Uncover and bake for an
  additional 25 minutes. Serve
  over rice. Serves 6 to 8.

Birds of a Feather Frys, Grills and Sautes

*Make your brood happy in a snap
with these quick and easy chicken sautés
and frys. Grilling never got any easier!*

Birds of a Feather Frys, Grills and Sautes Contents

Birds of a Feather Frys, Grills and Sautes Contents

American Chicken

2 cups cooked chicken breast halves, sliced in strips	280 g
1 cup sliced celery	100 g
1½ cups cooked rice	250 g
1 tablespoon butter	15 ml
2 tablespoons flour	15 g
1½ cups chicken broth	375 g

- Combine chicken and celery in bowl and mix with rice, 1 teaspoon (2 ml) salt and ⅛ teaspoon (.5 ml) pepper. Melt butter in skillet and make into smooth paste with flour.

- Add broth slowly and stir constantly. Bring to a boil and continue stirring.

- Add chicken and rice mixture and heat thoroughly. Serves 6.

Asparagus Chicken

1 (1 ounce) packet hollandaise sauce mix	30 g
2 large boneless skinless chicken breasts, cut into strips	
Olive oil	
1 tablespoon lemon juice	15 ml
1 (8 ounce) package egg noodles, cooked	230 g
1 (15 ounce) can asparagus spears	425 g

- Prepare hollandaise sauce according to package directions.

- Cook chicken strips in large skillet with a little oil for 12 to 15 minutes or until brown and stir occasionally.

- Add hollandaise sauce and lemon juice. Cover and cook for an additional 10 minutes, stirring occasionally.

- When ready to serve, place chicken over noodles and add hot asparagus spears. Serves 6.

Asparagus-Cheese Chicken

1 tablespoon butter	15 ml
4 boneless, skinless chicken breast halves	
1 (10 ounce) can broccoli-cheese soup	280 g
1 (10 ounce) package frozen asparagus cuts	280 g
⅓ cup milk	75 ml

- Heat butter in skillet and cook chicken for 10 to 15 minutes or until brown on both sides. Remove chicken and set aside.

- In same skillet, combine soup, asparagus and milk. Heat to boiling. Return chicken to skillet and reduce heat to low.

- Cover and cook for an additional 25 minutes until chicken is no longer pink and asparagus is tender. Serves 4.

Cheesy Chicken and Potatoes

1 (20 ounce) package frozen hash browns with peppers and onions, thawed	570 g
Olive oil	
1 tablespoon minced garlic	15 ml
2 - 2½ cups bite-size chunks rotisserie chicken	280 - 600 g
1 bunch green onions, sliced	
1 cup shredded cheddar cheese	115 g

- Cook potatoes in a little oil in large skillet over medium-high heat for 7 minutes and turn frequently.

- Add garlic, chicken, green onions and ⅓ cup (75 ml) water and cook for 5 to 6 minutes. Remove from heat and stir in cheese. Serve immediately right from skillet. Serves 8.

Chicken and Sauerkraut

**6 large, boneless, skinless
   chicken breast halves**
**1 (15 ounce) can sliced
   potatoes, drained   425 g**
**1 (16 ounce) can sauerkraut,
   drained   455 g**
¼ cup pine nuts   30 g

- Season chicken with a little black pepper and cook in large skillet over medium heat for 15 minutes or until chicken browns on both sides.

- Add potatoes to skillet and spoon sauerkraut over potatoes. Cover and cook over low heat for 35 minutes or until chicken is done.

- Toast pine nuts in dry skillet on medium heat until golden brown. Stir constantly. Sprinkle chicken and sauerkraut with toasted pine nuts and serve. Serves 6.

*TIP: This is good served with
        sour cream.*

Chicken and Shrimp Curry

**2 (10 ounce) cans
   cream of chicken
   soup   2 (280 g)**
⅓ cup milk   75 ml
**1½ teaspoons curry
   powder   7 ml**
**1 (12 ounce) can boned
   chicken   340 g**
**1 (6 ounce) can shrimp,
   drained, veined   170 g**
Rice, cooked

- Heat soup, milk and curry powder in saucepan. Stir in chicken pieces and shrimp.

- Serve over buttered rice. Serves 6.

Chicken and Wild Rice Special

1 (6 ounce) package long
    grain-wild rice mix   170 g
4 - 5 boneless, skinless
    chicken breast halves
Olive oil
2 (10 ounce) cans
    French onion soup   2 (280 g)
1 red bell pepper,
    julienned
1 green bell pepper, julienned

- Cook rice according to package directions in saucepan and keep warm. Brown chicken breasts in large skillet with a little oil over medium-high heat on both sides.

- Add soups, ¾ cup (175 ml) water and bell peppers. Reduce heat to medium-low, cover and cook for 15 minutes.

- To serve, place rice on serving platter with chicken breasts on top. Serve sauce in gravy boat to pour over chicken and rice. Serves 5.

TIP: *For a thicker sauce, spoon 2 or 3 tablespoons (30 to 45 ml) sauce in small bowl and stir in 2 tablespoons (15 g) flour. Mix well and stir in onion soup. Heat and stir constantly until sauce thickens.*

Q: *What do you call a frightened scuba diver?*

A: *Chicken of the sea.*

Chicken and the Works

6 boneless, skinless
   chicken breast halves
Olive oil
2 (10 ounce) cans cream
   of chicken soup   2 (280 g)
2 cups instant white rice   190 g
1 (10 ounce) package
   frozen green peas,
   thawed   280 g

- Sprinkle chicken with black pepper and brown in large, 12-inch (32 cm) skillet with a little oil. Reduce heat, cover and simmer for about 15 minutes. Transfer chicken to plate and keep warm.

- Add soup, 2 cups (500 ml) water and mix well. Heat to boiling and stir in rice and green peas. Top with chicken breasts, cover and simmer over low heat for about 10 minutes. Serves 6.

Chicken Cacciatore

1 (2½ pound) frying chicken   1.1 kg
Olive oil
2 onions, sliced
1 (15 ounce) can stewed
   tomatoes   425 g
1 (8 ounce) can tomato
   sauce   230 g
1 teaspoon dried oregano   5 ml
1 teaspoon celery seed   5 ml

- Quarter chicken and sprinkle with plenty of salt and black pepper. Place in large skillet on medium-high heat with a little oil. Add sliced onions and cook until chicken is tender, about 15 minutes.

- Add stewed tomatoes, tomato sauce, oregano and celery seed. Bring mixture to a boil, reduce heat and simmer for about 20 minutes. Serves 6.

TIP: *This is great over hot cooked noodles or spaghetti.*

Chicken Couscous

1 (5.6 ounce) package
   toasted pine nut
   couscous, cooked   160 g
1 rotisserie chicken,
   boned, cubed
1 (15 ounce) can baby
   green peas, drained   425 g
⅓ cup golden raisins   50 g

- Combine couscous, chicken, peas and raisins in microwave-safe dish. Heat on MEDIUM for about 2 minutes or until mixture is warm and stir once. Serves 6.

Chicken Curry

2 (10 ounce) cans cream
   of mushroom soup   2 (280 g)
2 teaspoons curry
   powder   10 ml
⅓ cup chopped
   almonds, toasted   65 g
4 boneless, skinless
   chicken breast halves,
   cooked, cubed
White rice, cooked

- Combine soups, 1 soup can water, curry powder, almonds and cubed chicken in large saucepan.

- Heat and stir frequently.

- When ready to serve, spoon over white rice. Serves 4.

Chicken Marseilles

3 tablespoons butter	35 g
5 - 6 boneless, skinless chicken breast halves	
1 (1 ounce) packet vegetable soup mix	30 g
½ teaspoon dill weed	2 ml
½ cup sour cream	120 g
Brown rice, cooked	

- Melt butter in skillet, brown chicken for about 10 to 15 minutes and turn occasionally.

- Stir 2 cups (500 ml) water, soup mix and dill weed into skillet and bring to a boil.

- Reduce heat, cover and simmer, stirring occasionally for 25 to 30 minutes or until chicken is tender.

- Remove chicken to hot plate, add sour cream to skillet and stir until creamy.

- Place chicken on hot brown rice and spoon sauce over chicken. Serves 6.

Chicken Elegant

This is rich, but worth the calories!

3 tablespoons butter	35 g
3 tablespoons flour	20 g
1¾ cups milk	425 g
½ cup shredded sharp cheddar cheese	60 g
½ cup shredded Swiss cheese	55 g
½ teaspoon Worcestershire sauce	2 ml
1 cup cooked, diced chicken or turkey	140 g
1 cup cooked, diced ham	140 g
1 (4 ounce) can sliced mushrooms, drained	115 g
2 tablespoons chopped pimento	30 ml
Noodles, cooked	

- Melt butter in saucepan and blend in flour. Add milk all at once, cook and stir until sauce is thick and bubbly. Remove from heat, add cheeses and stir until they melt.

- Stir in Worcestershire sauce, chicken or turkey, ham, mushrooms and pimento. Heat thoroughly and serve over noodles. Serves 8.

Chicken Fajitas

2 pounds boneless, skinless chicken breast halves	910 g
1 onion, thinly sliced	
1 red bell pepper, seeded, slice	
1 teaspoon ground cumin	5 ml
1½ teaspoons chili powder	7 ml
1 tablespoon lime juice	15 ml
½ cup chicken broth	125 ml
8 - 10 warmed flour tortillas	
Guacamole	
Sour cream	
Lettuce and tomatoes	

- Cut chicken into diagonal strips and place in large skillet. Add onion, bell pepper, cumin, chili powder, lime juice and chicken broth, cover and cook over medium heat for 25 minutes.

- When serving, spoon chicken mixture with sauce into center of each warm tortilla and fold.

- Serve with guacamole, sour cream, lettuce or tomatoes or plain. Serves 8.

Simple Chicken In Wine

¼ cup (½ stick) butter	60 g
4 large boneless, skinless chicken breast halves	
1 cup diced celery	100 g
½ cup seeded, diced green or red bell pepper	115 g
½ cup minced onion	80 g
1½ cups white wine	375 g

- Melt butter in large skillet over medium-high heat and brown chicken on all sides. Remove chicken and set aside.

- Saute celery, bell pepper and onion in saucepan until onion is translucent.

- Pour in wine and stir. Return chicken to skillet, cover and cook for about 1 hour or until juices run clear. Baste with pan juices several times while chicken cooks. Serves 4.

Chicken-Broccoli Skillet

3 cups cooked, cubed chicken	420 g
1 (16 ounce) package frozen broccoli florets	455 g
1 (8 ounce) package cubed Velveeta® cheese	230 g
⅔ cup mayonnaise	150 g
Rice, cooked	

- Combine chicken, broccoli, cheese and ¼ cup (60 ml) water in skillet.

- Cover and cook over medium heat until broccoli is tender-crisp and cheese melts.

- Stir in mayonnaise and heat through, but do not boil. Serve over rice. Serves 6.

Salsa-Grilled Chicken

4 - 5 boneless, skinless chicken beast halves	
1 cup thick-and-chunky salsa	265 g
¼ cup packed dark brown sugar	55 g
1 tablespoon dijon-style mustard	15 ml

- Pound chicken to about ½-inch (1.2 cm) thick. Combine remaining ingredients in large bowl. Add chicken to bowl, coat with marinade and marinate for 3 to 4 hours in refrigerator.

- Grill over hot coals until juices run clear. Serves 4 to 5.

Grilled Chicken with Raspberry-Barbecue Sauce

Raspberry-Barbecue Sauce:

1 (12 ounce) jar seedless raspberry preserves	340 g
½ cup bottled barbecue sauce	135 g
2 tablespoons raspberry vinegar	30 ml
2 tablespoons dijon-style mustard	30 g

Chicken:

1 (2½ pound) chicken, quartered	1.1 kg

- Combine all sauce ingredients in bowl and have ready when chicken quarters are nearly done.

- Season chicken quarters liberally with salt and pepper. Grill chicken, covered, over medium-high heat for about 8 minutes on each side. Baste Raspberry-Barbecue sauce over quarters during last 2 minutes of cooking.

- Serve with remaining sauce. Serves 8.

Americans eat an average of 80 pounds of chicken annually

Chicken-Orzo Supper

1 (5 ounce) box chicken-flavored orzo	145 g
1 (7 ounce) package cooked chicken strips	200 g
1 (10 ounce) package frozen corn	280 g
1 (10 ounce) package frozen cut green beans	280 g
¼ cup extra-virgin olive oil	60 ml
1 teaspoon minced garlic	5 ml

- Cook orzo according to package directions. Add chicken strips, corn, green beans, olive oil, garlic, ¼ cup (60 ml) water and a little salt and pepper and mix well.

- Cook on low heat and stir several times until mixture is hot, for about 10 to 15 minutes. Serves 4.

Alfredo-Chicken Spaghetti

1 (8 ounce) package thin spaghetti, broken in thirds	230 g
2 teaspoons minced garlic	10 ml
1 (16 ounce) jar alfredo sauce	455 g
¼ cup milk	60 ml
1 (10 ounce) box broccoli florets, thawed	280 g
2 cups cooked, diced chicken	280 g

- Cook spaghetti according to package directions and drain. Place back in saucepan and stir in garlic, alfredo sauce and milk and mix well.

- Add drained broccoli florets and cook on medium heat for about 5 minutes and stir several times or until broccoli is tender.

- Add more milk if mixture gets too dry. Stir in diced chicken and spoon into serving bowl. Serves 8.

Creamy Chicken and Broccoli

**5 large boneless, skinless
   chicken breast
   halves, thawed**
Olive oil
**2 (10 ounce) cans
   creamy chicken
   verde soup**   **2 (280 g)**
½ cup milk   **125 ml**
**1 (16 ounce) package
   frozen broccoli
   florets, thawed**   **455 g**
**2 cups cooked instant
   brown rice**   **390 g**

- Sprinkle chicken with salt and pepper and brown breasts in oil in large skillet with lid.

- Mix both cans soup and milk in saucepan. Cook over medium heat until soups and milk mix thoroughly. Stir frequently.

- Ladle soup mixture over top of chicken; reduce heat, cover and simmer for 20 minutes.

- Place broccoli around chicken and return heat to high until broccoli is hot. Reduce heat and simmer for about 10 minutes. Serve chicken and sauce over brown rice. Serves 5.

What do you get when you cross a chick with an alley cat?

A peeping tom.

Almond Chicken

4 boneless, skinless chicken
   breasts halves
3 tablespoons butter   35 g
1 (6 ounce) can frozen
   orange juice
   concentrate, thawed   170 g
2 tablespoons bourbon   30 ml
Rice, cooked
½ cup chopped, salted
   almonds, toasted   45 g

• Brown chicken in butter in skillet over medium heat and reduce heat to low. Add orange juice, ½ teaspoon (2 ml) salt and ¼ teaspoon (1 ml) pepper.

• Cover and cook over medium heat for 25 minutes. Spoon sauce over chicken twice while it cooks. Remove chicken to serving platter and keep warm.

• Add bourbon to sauce in skillet, stir and heat. Pour mixture over chicken and serve over rice. Sprinkle with almonds. Serves 4.

Creamy Mushroom Chicken

4 boneless, skinless chicken
   breast halves
Olive oil
1 (10 ounce) can cream of
   mushroom soup   280 g
1 (4 ounce) cans sliced
   mushrooms, drained   115 g
½ cup milk   125 ml

• Sprinkle chicken liberally with a little salt and pepper. Brown chicken on both sides with a little oil in skillet over high heat.

• While chicken browns, combine mushroom soup, mushrooms and milk in saucepan and heat jut enough to mix well.

• Pour over chicken breasts, reduce heat to low and simmer covered for 15 minutes. Serves 4.

Grilled Chicken with Broccoli Slaw

Chicken:

1 (3½ pound) chicken, quartered	1.6 kg
3 tablespoons olive oil	45 ml
⅔ cup bottled barbecue sauce	180 g

- Brush chicken quarters with oil and sprinkle with salt and pepper.

- Grill for 30 to 35 minutes, turning once or twice or until juices run clear when thigh part is pierced and a meat thermometer inserted registers 175° (80° C).

- Brush with barbecue sauce and grill just until sauce is brown, but not charred.

Slaw:

¼ cup mayonnaise	55 g
3 tablespoons cider vinegar	45 ml
2 tablespoons sugar	25 g
1 (12 ounce) package broccoli slaw	340 g

- Combine mayonnaise, vinegar and sugar in bowl and mix well. Spoon over broccoli slaw and toss. Refrigerate until ready to serve. Serves 6 to 8.

Crunchy Chip Chicken

**1½ cups crushed sour cream
  potato chips**   **85 g**
1 tablespoon dried parsley   **15 ml**
1 egg, beaten
**1 tablespoon Worcestershire
  sauce**   **15 ml**
**4 large boneless, skinless
  chicken breast halves**
¼ cup olive oil   **60 ml**

- Combine potato chips and parsley in shallow bowl.

- In separate shallow bowl, combine beaten egg, Worcestershire and 1 tablespoon (15 ml) water.

- Dip chicken pieces in egg mixture and dredge chicken in potato chip mixture. Heat oil in heavy skillet and fry chicken pieces in skillet for about 10 minutes.

- Turn each piece over and cook for an additional 10 minutes until golden brown or until juices run clear. Serves 4.

A chicken can travel up to 9 miles an hour.

Dijon Skillet Chicken

¼ cup ranch salad dressing	60 ml
1 tablespoon dijon-style mustard	15 ml
4 boneless, skinless chicken breast halves	
2 tablespoons butter	30 g
3 tablespoons white wine or chicken broth	45 ml
Rice, cooked	

- Combine salad dressing and mustard in salad bowl and set aside.

- Cook chicken in butter in skillet and simmer for 10 to 15 minutes.

- Add wine or broth and simmer for an additional 20 minutes.

- Whisk in mustard mixture, cook and stir until it blends and is thoroughly hot. Serve over rice. Serves 4.

Deep-Fried Chicken

1 whole chicken, cut up	
1 cup flour	120 g
2 eggs	
2 cups milk	500 ml
1 teaspoon lemon juice	5 ml

- Wash and pat dry chicken with paper towels. Season chicken with a little salt and pepper. Combine flour, eggs, milk and lemon juice in bowl and mix thoroughly.

- Dredge chicken in batter and fry in deep fryer over medium-high heat until golden brown. Serves 6.

Creamy Tarragon Chicken

1½ cups flour	180 g
6 boneless, skinless chicken breast halves	
2 tablespoons oil	30 ml
1 (14 ounce) can chicken broth	400 g
1 cup milk	250 ml
2 teaspoons dried tarragon	10 ml
1 (4 ounce) can sliced mushrooms, drained	115 g
2 (8 ounce) packages roasted chicken flavored rice	2 (230 g)

- Mix flour and a little salt and pepper on wax paper and coat chicken. Save extra flour.

- Heat oil in large skillet over medium-high heat and cook chicken breasts, turning once for about 10 minutes or until light brown. Transfer to plate.

- In same skillet, stir in 2 tablespoons (15 g) flour-salt mixture. Whisk in chicken broth, milk and tarragon, heat and stir constantly until bubbly. Add mushrooms and return chicken to skillet.

- Cover and simmer for 10 to 15 minutes or until sauce thickens. Microwave rice in package according to package directions and place on serving platter. Spoon chicken and sauce over rice. Serves 6.

Easy Green Chile Chicken

6 boneless, skinless chicken
    breast halves
Flour
Olive oil
1 onion, chopped
2 ribs celery, chopped
3 tablespoons white wine
    vinegar   **45 ml**
4 tablespoons
    Worcestershire sauce **60 ml**
1 cup white wine   **250 ml**
1 (7 ounce) can chopped
    green chilies   **200 g**
Rice, cooked

- Season chicken with salt and pepper. Dredge chicken in flour, brown in hot oil in skillet and remove from heat.

- Combine onion, celery, vinegar, Worcestershire, wine and green chilies in bowl and mix well. Pour mixture over chicken in skillet, cover and cook for about 30 to 45 minutes.

- Uncover and cook until chicken juices are clear and chicken breasts are slightly brown. Serve over rice. Serves 6 to 8.

According to the National Geographic, scientists have settled the old dispute over which came first – the chicken or the egg. They say that reptiles were laying eggs thousands of years before chickens appeared, and the first chicken came from an egg laid by a bird that was not quite a chicken. Clearly, the egg came first.

Fried Chicken Breasts

4 boneless, skinless chicken breast halves
2 eggs, beaten
20 saltine crackers, crushed

- Pound chicken breasts to ¼-inch (6 mm) thickness.

- Combine eggs, ¼ teaspoon (1 ml) pepper and 2 tablespoons (30 ml) water.

- Dip chicken in egg mixture then in crushed crackers and coat well. Deep fry until golden brown and drain well. Serves 4.

Fried Chicken Livers

1 pound chicken livers, washed, dried　　455 g
2 tablespoons milk　　30 ml
2 eggs, beaten
Flour
Canola oil

- Season chicken livers with pepper. Add milk to beaten eggs and dip livers into egg mixture. Roll in flour and coat livers well.

- Heat about ¼-inch (6 mm) oil in heavy skillet and brown livers on both sides. Lower heat and cook until tender, for about 15 to 20 minutes.

- Remove from skillet, drain on paper towels, salt and pepper again and serve immediately. Serves 4.

Glazed Chicken and Rice

4 boneless, skinless chicken
    breast halves, cubed
Olive oil
1 (20 ounce) can pineapple
    chunks with juice   570 g
½ cup honey-mustard
    grill-and-glaze sauce   135 g
1 red bell pepper, chopped
1 cup cooked instant rice   165 g

- Brown chicken in skillet with a little oil and cook over low heat for 15 minutes. Add pineapple, honey-mustard sauce and bell pepper and bring to a boil.

- Reduce heat to low and simmer for 10 to 15 minutes or until sauce thickens slightly. Serve over rice. Serves 8.

Grilled Chicken Cordon Bleu

6 boneless, skinless chicken
    breast halves
6 slices Swiss cheese
6 thin slices deli ham
3 tablespoons olive oil   45 ml
1 cup seasoned
    breadcrumbs   120 g

- Flatten chicken to ¼-inch (6 mm) thickness and place 1 slice cheese and ham on each piece of chicken to within ¼-inch (6 mm) of edges.

- Fold in half and secure with toothpicks. Brush chicken with oil and roll in breadcrumbs.

- Grill covered over medium-hot heat for 15 to 18 minutes or until juices run clear. Serves 6.

Grilled Chicken Fajitas

6 boneless, skinless chicken breast halves
¼ cup sesame seeds   **30 g**
⅛ teaspoon cayenne pepper   **.5 ml**
1 red or green bell pepper
1 onion
12 flour tortillas, warmed

- Pound chicken breasts between pieces of wax paper to flatten. Sprinkle both sides of chicken breasts with sesame seeds, cayenne pepper and salt.

- Slice bell pepper into strips and slice onion twice to make 3 thick slices.

- Grill chicken breasts, bell pepper and onion over charcoal fire. Cook for about 5 minutes on each side. Cut chicken breasts into thin strips.

- To assemble, place several strips chicken, bell pepper and onion in center of tortilla. Fold over and serve. Serves 6.

TIP: *Traditional fajitas do not include sour cream, guacamole or chopped avocado, but you don't have to be traditional.*

Gourmet Chicken

2 small chickens, skinned,
    quartered
Flour
Olive oil
1 (15 ounce) can sliced
    pineapple with juice   425 g
1 cup sugar   200 g
3 tablespoons cornstarch   25 g
¾ cup vinegar   175 ml
1 tablespoon soy sauce   15 ml
¼ teaspoon ground ginger   1 ml
2 chicken bouillon cubes
1 tablespoon lemon juice   15 ml
2 bell peppers, cut in strips
White rice, cooked

- Preheat oven to 350° (175° C).

- Wash chicken and pat dry with paper towel. Coat chicken with salt, pepper and flour. Brown chicken quarters in oil and place in sprayed 10 x 15-inch (25 x 38 cm) roasting pan.

- To make sauce, drain pineapple syrup into 2-cup measure. Add water (or orange juice) to make 1½ cups (375 ml).

- Combine sugar, cornstarch, pineapple syrup, vinegar, soy sauce, ginger, bouillon cubes and lemon juice in medium saucepan and bring to a boil.

- Stir constantly for about 2 minutes or until sauce thickens and becomes clear. Pour over browned chicken. Cover and bake for about 40 minutes.

- Place pineapple slices and bell pepper on top of chicken and bake for 10 to 15 minutes longer. Serve over rice. Serves 8.

Grilled Lemon Chicken

2 teaspoons garlic salt	10 ml
1 tablespoon freshly grated lemon peel	15 ml
2 teaspoons dried thyme leaves	10 ml
6 boneless, skinless chicken breast halves	

- Combine garlic salt, lemon peel, thyme leaves and a little pepper in small bowl. Heat coals and spray grill.

- Sprinkle seasoning mixture over chicken breasts. Grill chicken for 20 to 25 minutes or until chicken is no longer pink and juices run clear. Turn once during cooking. Serves 6.

Italian Chicken and Rice

3 boneless, chicken breasts halves, cut into strips	
1 (14 ounce) can chicken broth seasoned with Italian herbs	400 g
¾ cup rice	70 g
¼ cup grated parmesan cheese	25 g

- Cook chicken in non-stick skillet until brown, stirring often and set aside.

- Add broth and rice to skillet and heat to boil. Cover and simmer over low heat for 25 minutes. (Add water if necessary.)

- Stir in cheese and return chicken to pan. Cover and cook for 5 minutes or until done. Serves 6.

Italian Chicken over Couscous

1 pound frozen chicken tenders, halved	455 g
Olive oil	
1 onion, chopped	
1 (15 ounce) can Italian stewed tomatoes	425 g
⅔ cup pitted kalamata olives	85 g
1 (5.8 ounce) box roasted garlic and olive oil couscous	170 g

- Season chicken with a little salt and pepper. Place in large skillet with a little oil.

- Add onion and chicken, cook and cover over medium-high heat for about 8 minutes and turn once. Add tomatoes and olives, cover and cook for an additional 8 minutes.

- Prepare couscous according to package directions.

- Spoon couscous onto serving plates and top with chicken and sauce. Serves 8.

Jambalaya

1 (8 ounce) package jambalaya mix	230 g
1 (6 ounce) package frozen chicken breast strips, thawed	170 g
1 (11 ounce) can Mexicorn®	310 g
1 (2 ounce) can chopped black olives	60 g
Rice, cooked	

- Combine jambalaya mix and 2¼ cups (560 ml) water in soup pot or large saucepan. Heat to boiling, reduce heat and cook slowly for 5 minutes.

- Add chicken, corn and black olives. Heat to boiling, reduce heat and simmer for about 20 minutes. Serve over rice. Serves 6.

TIP: *You could also add leftover ham or sausage and 1 tablespoon (15 ml) lemon juice to change it up some. If you want to serve more than 6 people, just double the recipe.*

Lemony Chicken and Noodles

1 (8 ounce) package wide egg noodles	230 g
1 (10 ounce) package frozen sugar snap peas, thawed	280 g
1 (14 ounce) can chicken broth	400 g
1 teaspoon fresh grated lemon peel	5 ml
2 cups cubed, skinless rotisserie chicken meat	280 g
½ cup whipping cream	125 ml

- Cook noodles in large saucepan with boiling water according to package directions, but add snap peas to noodles 1 minute before noodles are done. Drain and return to saucepan.

- Add chicken broth, lemon peel, chicken pieces and ½ teaspoon (2 ml) each of salt and pepper. Heat, stirring constantly, until thoroughly hot.

- Gently stir in whipping cream over low heat. Serve hot. Serves 8.

Lime-Salsa Campsite Chicken

¼ cup oil	60 ml
1 (10 ounce) jar green chile salsa	280 g
1½ tablespoons lime juice	22 ml
½ teaspoon sugar	2 ml
1 teaspoon garlic powder	5 ml
1 teaspoon ground cumin	5 ml
½ teaspoon oregano	2 ml
6 boneless, skinless chicken breast halves	

- Combine all ingredients except chicken in bowl and mix well. Add chicken breasts and marinate for 3 to 4 hours.

- Cook over hot coals for about 10 to 15 minutes or until juices run clear. Turn occasionally. Serves 6.

Mandarin Chicken

1 (11 ounce) can mandarin oranges, drained	310 g
1 (6 ounce) can frozen orange juice concentrate	170 g
1 tablespoon lemon juice	15 ml
1 tablespoon cornstarch	15 ml
4 boneless, skinless chicken breast halves	
2 tablespoons garlic-and-herb seasoning	30 ml
2 tablespoons butter	30 g

- Combine oranges, orange juice concentrate, lemon juice, ⅔ cup (150 ml) water and cornstarch in saucepan. Cook on medium heat, stirring constantly, until mixture thickens. Set aside.

- Sprinkle chicken breasts with seasoning and place in skillet with butter. Cook for about 7 minutes on each side until brown.

- Lower heat and spoon orange juice mixture over chicken, cover, simmer for about 20 minutes and add a little water if sauce gets too thick. Serves 4.

Maple-Plum Glazed Turkey Breast

2 cups red plum jam	640 g
1 cup maple syrup	250 ml
1 teaspoon dry mustard	5 ml
¼ cup lemon juice	60 ml
1 (5 pound) bone-in turkey breast	2.2 kg

- Combine plum jam, syrup, mustard and lemon juice in saucepan and bring to a boil.

- Turn down heat and simmer for about 20 minutes or until glaze is thick. Set aside 1 cup of glaze (250 ml).

- Place turkey breast in roasting pan, pour remaining glaze over turkey and bake according to directions on turkey package.

- Slice turkey and serve with heated, set aside glaze. Serves 8.

Creamy Chicken and Mushrooms

½ cup (1 stick) butter	115 g
1 (1½ pound) carton fresh mushrooms, sliced	680 g
3 cups cooked, cubed chicken	420 g
⅓ cup flour	40 g
2 (14 ounce) cans chicken broth	2 (400 g)
½ cup sherry	125 ml
Cayenne pepper	

- Melt butter in large skillet over medium-high heat and saute mushrooms. Add chicken and cook for 3 to 4 minutes. Add flour, stir well to remove lumps and slowly pour in broth while stirring.

- Reduce heat and simmer for about 10 to 15 minutes. Add sherry and cayenne pepper just before serving. Serves 8.

Hurry-Up Chicken Enchiladas

2½ - 3 cups cooked, cubed chicken breasts	350 - 420 g
1 (10 ounce) can cream of chicken soup	280 g
1½ cups chunky salsa, divided	395 g
8 (6 inch) flour tortillas	8 (15 cm)
1 (10 ounce) can fiesta nacho cheese soup	280 g

- Combine chicken, soup and ½ cup (130 g) salsa in saucepan and heat.

- Spoon about ⅓ cup (50 g) chicken mixture down center of each tortilla and roll tortilla around filling. Place seam-side down in sprayed 9 x 13-inch (23 x 33 cm) baking dish.

- Mix nacho cheese, remaining salsa and ¼ cup (60 ml) water and pour over enchiladas. Cover with wax paper and microwave on HIGH, turning several times for 5 minutes. Serves 8.

Mole con Pollo y Arroz

Mole is a traditional Mexican sauce well known all over the world. Chocolate is the secret ingredient used to make the sauce rich, but not overly sweet.

1 cup chopped onion	160 g
Olive oil	
2 cloves garlic, chopped	
1 cup slivered almonds	170 g
1 (1 ounce) square bittersweet chocolate	30 g
1 (15 ounce) can tomato sauce	425 g
2 (7 ounce) cans green chile salsa	2 (200 g)
2 cups cooked, chopped chicken	280 g
1 cup cooked rice	165 g
Avocado	
Lime	
Sour cream	

- Heat a little oil in skillet and cook onion, garlic and almonds until onions are translucent.

- Add ¼ teaspoon (1 ml) pepper and chocolate and heat on low until chocolate melts. Stir constantly.

- Pour tomato sauce, green chile salsa and chocolate mixture into blender and process until smooth.

- Pour sauce in skillet and add chicken. Stir to mix well and simmer for about 5 to 10 minutes.

- Serve over hot rice and garnish with avocado and lime slices and dollop of sour cream. Serves 8.

TIP: *Mole is a smooth, rich, dark red sauce usually containing a blend of garlic, onion and various chiles and seeds, such as pumpkin seeds called pepitas. A small amount of chocolate makes the sauce a richer flavor and color without adding a sweet flavor.*

Quick Tex-Mex Supper

12 corn tortillas
1 (12 ounce) package
    shredded Mexican
    4-cheese blend,
    divided   **340 g**
2 (12 ounce) cans
    chicken breasts,
    drained, shredded   **2 (340 g)**
1 small onion, chopped
2 (10 ounce) cans
    enchilada sauce   **2 (280 g)**

- Wrap 6 tortillas in slightly damp paper towel. Place between 2 salad plates and microwave on HIGH for 30 to 40 seconds.

- On each tortilla, place about ⅓ cup (38 g) cheese, chicken and 1 tablespoon (15 ml) onion and roll. Repeat steps with remaining tortillas.

- Place tortillas seam-side down on sprayed 10 x 15-inch (25 x 38 cm) baking dish and pour enchilada sauce on top.

- Sprinkle with remaining cheese and onions, cover and microwave on MEDIUM for 5 to 6 minutes. (If microwave does not have turntable, turn tortillas once during cooking.) Serves 8.

Skillet Chicken and More

4 boneless, skinless chicken
　　breast halves
Olive oil
2 (10 ounce) cans cream
　　of chicken soup　　2 (280 g)
2 cups instant white rice　190 g
1 (16 ounce) package
　　frozen broccoli
　　florets　　455 g

- Brown chicken breasts on both sides in very large skillet with a little oil and simmer for 10 minutes. Remove chicken and keep warm.

- Add soup and 2 cups (500 ml) water. Heat to boiling.

- Stir in instant rice and broccoli florets. Use a little salt and pepper on chicken and place on top of rice. Cover and cook on low for 15 minutes. Serves 4.

Savory Chicken and Mushrooms

1 (16 ounce) package frozen
　　chopped onions
　　and peppers　　455 g
1 (8 ounce) package fresh
　　mushrooms, sliced　　230 g
Olive oil
1 (10 ounce) can cream of
　　mushrooms soup　　280 g
1 cup milk　　250 ml
1 rotisserie chicken, boned
Rice, cooked

- Cook onions and peppers, and mushrooms in large skillet with a little oil for about 5 minutes or until onions are translucent and stir frequently.

- Stir in mushroom soup and milk, mix well and add chicken pieces and seasonings.

- Boil, reduce heat and cook for about 10 minutes. Serve over rice. Serves 8.

Skillet Chicken and Peas

Olive oil
4 - 5 boneless, skinless
   chicken breast halves
2 (10 ounce) can cream
   of chicken soup   2 (280 g)
2 cups instant rice   190 g
1 (10 ounce) package
   frozen green peas   280 g

- Heat a little oil in very large skillet. Add chicken and cook until it browns well. Transfer chicken to plate and keep warm.

- In same skillet, add soup, 1¾ cups (425 ml) water and about ½ teaspoon (2 ml) pepper. Heat to boiling, stir in rice and peas and reduce heat. Place chicken on top and cook on low heat for 15 minutes. Serves 5.

Skillet Chicken and Stuffing

1 (6 ounce) box chicken
   stuffing mix with
   seasoning packet   170 g
1 (16 ounce) package
   frozen corn   455 g
¼ cup (½ stick) butter   115 g
4 boneless, skinless chicken
   breast halves, cooked

- Combine contents of seasoning packet, corn, butter and 1⅔ (400 ml) cups water in large skillet and bring to a boil.

- Reduce heat, cover and simmer for 5 minutes.

- Stir in stuffing mix just until moist. Cut chicken into thin slices and mix with stuffing-corn mixture. Cook on low heat just until mixture heats well. Serves 4.

Classic Chicken Piccata

5 - 6 boneless, skinless
**   chicken breast halves**
Flour
Olive oil
3 tablespoons butter   35 g
1 clove garlic, minced
1 (1 pound) fresh
**   mushrooms, sliced   455 g**
1 (14 ounce) can chicken
**   broth   400 g**
½ cup dry white wine   125 ml
1 lemon
2 tablespoons capers   30 ml

• Rinse chicken pieces, pat dry and flatten to about ¼-inch (6 mm) thick with rolling pin. Dredge in flour and coat well.

• Pour a little oil and butter in large skillet and heat over medium-high heat. Place chicken in skillet and brown on all sides. Remove from skillet and keep warm.

• Saute garlic and mushrooms until tender. Add broth, wine and 3 to 4 tablespoons (45 ml) lemon juice and simmer for several minutes.

• Return chicken to skillet and coat with liquid. Add capers and simmer until chicken is done and juices run clear. Serves 5 to 6.

Southern Fried Chicken

1 whole chicken, cut up
2 eggs, beaten
2 tablespoons cream   **30 ml**
Flour
Olive oil or shortening

- Salt and pepper each piece of chicken. Combine beaten eggs and cream in bowl, dip chicken into mixture and roll in flour. Coat chicken well.

- Heat about ¼-inch (6 mm) oil or shortening in heavy skillet and brown chicken on both sides. Lower heat and cook for 25 minutes or until tender.

Gravy:

3 tablespoons flour   **20 g**
1½ cups milk   **375 ml**

- Remove chicken from skillet and add flour and ½ teaspoon (2 ml) each of salt and pepper. Stir and increase heat to high. Add milk and cook. Stir until gravy thickens. Serve hot. Serves 6.

Laid head to claw, KFC chickens consumed worldwide would stretch about 275,000 miles, circling the earth at the equator 11 times.

Stir-Fry Chicken Spaghetti

1 pound boneless, skinless chicken breast halves	455 g
Olive oil	
1½ cups sliced mushrooms	110 g
1½ cups bell pepper strips	140 g
1 cup sweet-and-sour stir-fry sauce	250 ml
1 (16 ounce) package spaghetti, cooked	455 g
¼ cup (½ stick) butter	60 g

- Season chicken with salt and pepper and cut into thin slices. Brown chicken slices in large skillet with a little oil and cook for 5 minutes on medium-low heat. Transfer to plate and set aside.

- In same skillet with a little more oil, stir-fry mushrooms and bell pepper strips for 5 minutes. Add chicken strips and sweet-and-sour sauce and stir until ingredients are hot.

- Cook spaghetti according to package directions, drain well, add butter and stir until butter melts. Place in large bowl and toss with chicken mixture. Serve hot. Serves 5.

Mary: Why does your son say "Cluck, cluck cluck?"

Jennifer: "Because he thinks he's a chicken."

Mary: "Why don't you tell him he's not a chicken?"

Jennifer: "Because we need the eggs."

Spaghetti Toss

1 (10 ounce) package thin spaghetti	280 g
1 (10 ounce) package frozen sugar snap peas	280 g
2 tablespoons butter	28 g
3 cups rotisserie-cooked chicken	420 g
1 (11 ounce) can mandarin oranges, drained	310 g
⅔ cup stir-fry sauce	150 ml

- Cook spaghetti according to package directions. Stir in sugar snap peas and cook for an additional minute.

- Drain and stir in butter until butter melts. Spoon into bowl. Cut chicken into strips and add strips, oranges and stir-fry sauce. Toss to coat. Serves 8.

Chicken Kick

1 tablespoon paprika	15 ml
1 teaspoon ground cumin	5 ml
½ teaspoon cayenne pepper	2 ml
½ teaspoon coriander	2 ml
½ teaspoon oregano	2 ml
4 - 5 boneless, skinless chicken breasts, halved lengthwise	
Extra-virgin olive oil	

- Combine paprika, cumin, cayenne pepper, coriander, oregano and 1 teaspoon (5 ml) salt in small bowl.

- Place chicken pieces in large shallow baking dish and drizzle with olive oil to coat. Rub each piece with spice mix and let stand for about 10 minutes.

- Brown chicken pieces in large skillet over medium-high heat. Reduce heat, cover and simmer for about 10 minutes on each side. Transfer to serving platter. Serves 6 to 8.

Kicky Chicken

1 tablespoon paprika	15 ml
1 teaspoon ground cumin	5 ml
½ teaspoon cayenne pepper	2 ml
½ teaspoon coriander	2 ml
½ teaspoon oregano	2 ml
4 - 5 boneless, skinless chicken breasts, halved lengthwise	
Extra-virgin olive oil	

- Combine paprika, cumin, cayenne pepper, coriander, oregano and 1 teaspoon (5 ml) salt in small bowl.

- Place chicken pieces in large shallow baking dish and drizzle with olive oil to coat. Rub each piece with spice mix and let stand for about 10 minutes.

- Brown chicken pieces in large skillet over medium-high heat. Reduce heat, cover and simmer for about 10 minutes on each side. Transfer to serving platter. Serves 5.

Stir-Fry Chicken

Olive oil	
1 pound chicken tenders, cut into strips	455 g
1 (16 ounce) package frozen broccoli, cauliflower and carrots	455 g
1 (8 ounce) jar stir-fry sauce	230 g
1 (12 ounce) package chow mein noodles	340 g

- Place a little oil and stir-fry chicken strips in 12-inch (32 cm) wok over high heat for about 4 minutes.

- Add vegetables and stir-fry for an additional 4 minutes or until vegetables are tender. Stir in stir-fry sauce and cook just until mixture is hot. Serve over chow mein noodles. Serves 8.

Sunny Chicken Supper

4 boneless, skinless chicken breast halves	
1½ teaspoons curry powder	7 ml
1½ cups orange juice	375 ml
1 tablespoon brown sugar	15 ml
1 cup rice	95 g
1 teaspoon mustard	5 ml

• Rub chicken breasts with curry powder and a little salt and pepper. Combine orange juice, brown sugar, rice and mustard in large skillet and mix well.

• Place chicken breasts on top of rice mixture and bring to a boil. Reduce heat, cover and simmer for 30 minutes. Remove from heat and let stand, covered for about 10 minutes until all liquid absorbs into rice. Serves 4.

Sweet 'n Spicy Chicken

1 pound boneless, skinless chicken breast halves	455 g
1 (1 ounce) packet taco seasoning	30 g
Olive oil	
1 (16 ounce) jar chunky salsa	455 g
1 cup peach preserves	320 g
Rice or noodles, cooked	

• Cut chicken into ½-inch (1.2 cm) cubes. Place chicken in large, resealable plastic bag, add taco seasoning and toss to coat.

• Brown chicken in skillet with a little oil. Combine salsa and preserves in bowl, stir into skillet and bring mixture to a boil.

• Reduce heat, cover and simmer until juices run clear. Serve over rice or noodles. Serves 4.

Tempting Chicken

3 boneless, skinless chicken
    breast halves
3 boneless, skinless chicken
    thighs
Olive oil
1 (16 ounce) jar
    tomato-alfredo sauce   455 g
1 (10 ounce) can tomato
    bisque soup   280 g

- Brown chicken pieces in large skillet with a little oil.

- Heat tomato-alfredo sauce, tomato bisque soup and ½ cup (125 ml) water in saucepan just enough to mix. Pour over chicken.

- Cover and simmer for about 30 minutes. Serves 6.

Tasty Skillet Chicken

5 large boneless, skinless
    chicken breast halves
Olive oil
1 green bell pepper, julienned
1 red bell pepper, julienned
2 small yellow squash, seeded,
    julienned
1 (16 ounce) bottle
    thick-and-chunky salsa   455 g
Rice, cooked

- Cut chicken breasts into thin strips. Saute chicken in large skillet with a little oil for about 5 minutes. Add peppers and squash and cook for an additional 5 minutes or until peppers are tender-crisp.

- Stir in salsa and bring to a boil, lower heat and simmer for 10 minutes. Serve over rice. Serves 5.

Tequila-Lime Chicken

½ cup lime juice	125 ml
¼ cup tequila	60 ml
1½ teaspoons chili powder	7 ml
1½ teaspoons minced garlic	7 ml
1 teaspoon seeded jalapeno pepper	5 ml
6 boneless, chicken breast halves with skin	

- Combine all ingredients in large resealable plastic bag except chicken. Add chicken breasts, seal bag and turn to coat. Refrigerate for 10 hours or overnight.

- Remove breasts from marinade and sprinkle chicken with a little salt and pepper. Discard marinade.

- Grill skin-side down for 5 to 7 minutes. Turn and grill for 10 minutes or until it cooks thoroughly. Remove to platter, cover and let stand for 5 minutes before serving. Serves 6.

Turkey-Asparagus Alfredo

1 bunch fresh asparagus	
1 red bell pepper, julienned	
1 (16 ounce) jar alfredo sauce	455 g
½ pound smoked turkey, cut into strips	230 g

- Bring ½ cup (125 ml) water to boiling in large skillet. Cut off woody ends of asparagus and cut into thirds. Add asparagus and bell pepper to skillet, cook on medium-high heat for 4 minutes or until tender-crisp and drain.

- Stir in alfredo sauce and turkey strips. Bring to a boil, reduce heat and simmer until mixture is thoroughly hot. Serves 6.

Tortellini Supper

1 (9 ounce) package refrigerated cheese tortellini	255 g
1 (10 ounce) package frozen green peas, thawed	280 g
1 (8 ounce) carton cream cheese with chives and onion	230 g
½ cup sour cream	120 g
1 (9 ounce) package frozen cooked chicken breasts	255 g

- Cook cheese tortellini in saucepan according to package directions. Place peas in colander and pour hot pasta water over green peas. Return tortellini and peas to saucepan.

- Combine cream cheese and sour cream in smaller saucepan and heat on low, stirring well until cheese melts. Spoon mixture over tortellini and peas and toss with heat on low.

- Heat cooked chicken in microwave according to package directions. Spoon tortellini and peas in serving bowl and place chicken on top. Serve hot. Serves 6.

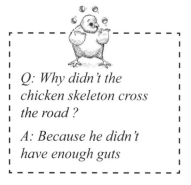

Q: Why didn't the chicken skeleton cross the road ?

A: Because he didn't have enough guts

Texas Chicken Fajitas

6 boneless, skinless chicken
    breast halves
Flour tortillas

Marinade:

1 cup salsa	265 g
1 cup Italian salad dressing	250 ml
2 tablespoons lemon juice	30 ml
2 tablespoons chopped green onions	30 ml
1 teaspoon garlic powder	5 ml
1 teaspoon celery salt	5 ml

Fillings for Fajitas:

Salsa
Guacamole
Grilled onions
Chopped tomatoes
Grated cheese
Sour cream

- Combine all marinade ingredients with 1 teaspoon (5 ml) pepper in bowl and mix well. Remove fat from meat and wipe dry with paper towels.

- Place meat in shallow dish and pour marinade over meat. Marinate overnight or for at least 6 hours in refrigerator.

- Drain liquid and cook over hot charcoal. Cut meat diagonally. Place a few meat strips on warmed flour tortilla, choose fillings, roll and eat! Serves 8.

Turkey Croquettes

These are very easy to make.
Make several batches and
freeze them for another meal.

1½ cups cooked, chopped turkey	**210 g**
1 (10 ounce) can cream of chicken soup	**280 g**
1 cup turkey stuffing mix	**35 g**
2 eggs	
1 tablespoon minced onion	**15 ml**
Flour	
Canola oil	

- Mix all ingredients in bowl and refrigerate for several hours. Shape into patties or rolls. Dredge in flour and fry in deep fat until brown. Serves 6.

Wild Rice and Chicken

1 (6 ounce) package long grain-wild rice mix	**170 g**
4 boneless, skinless chicken breast halves	
½ cup (1 stick) butter, divided	**115 g**
1 large red bell pepper, chopped	

- Prepare rice according to package directions.

- Cook chicken in 2 tablespoons (30 g) butter in large skillet and make sure each chicken breast browns on both sides. Remove chicken and keep warm.

- Add remaining butter to pan drippings and saute red bell pepper until tender. Add to rice. Serve with cooked chicken breasts. Serves 4.

Turkey and Rice Olé

This may be served as a 1-dish meal or as a sandwich wrap in flour tortillas.

1 pound ground turkey	455 g
1 (5.5 ounce) package Mexican rice mix	155 g
1 (15 ounce) can black beans, rinsed, drained	425 g
1 cup thick-and-chunky salsa	265 g

- Brown turkey in large skillet and break up large pieces with fork. Add rice mix and 2 cups (500 ml) water.

- Bring to a boil, reduce heat and simmer for about 8 minutes or until rice is tender. Stir in beans and salsa and cook just until mixture is hot. Serves 6.

Dad's Best Smoked Chicken

3 whole chickens, cut in half	
½ cup (1 stick) butter	115 g
2 teaspoons Worcestershire sauce	10 ml
2 dashes hot sauce	
2 tablespoons lemon juice	30 ml
½ teaspoon garlic salt	2 ml
1 (12 ounce) can lemon-lime carbonated drink	340 g

- Sprinkle chickens with pepper and leave at room temperature for 1 hour. Melt butter in small saucepan and add Worcestershire sauce, hot sauce, lemon juice and garlic salt and add carbonated drink.

- Cook chickens over low charcoal fire with hickory or mesquite chips around sides of fire. Turn often and baste with sauce mixture several times.

- When chicken is done (about 60 minutes), baste once more to keep chicken moist. Serves 12.

Yummy Barbecued-Grilled Chicken

**6 boneless, skinless chicken
   breast halves**

3 cups ketchup	**815 g**
½ cup packed brown sugar	**110 g**
¼ cup Worcestershire sauce	**60 ml**
2 tablespoons vinegar	**30 ml**
1 teaspoon hot sauce	**5 ml**

- Wash and dry chicken breasts with paper towels. Combine ketchup, brown sugar, Worcestershire sauce, vinegar, 2 teaspoons (10 ml) salt, hot sauce and ½ teaspoon (2 ml) pepper in saucepan and mix well.

- Bring to a boil, reduce heat to low and cook for 15 minutes.

- Fire up grill and smoke chicken over mesquite wood, if possible. Baste chicken frequently with barbecue sauce. Turn chicken periodically and cook chicken 8 to 10 minutes per side or until juices are clear.

- Any leftover barbecue sauce keeps well in refrigerator. Serves 6.

When grilling out, clean the grill well before each use to prevent bacterial contamination.

Texas-Pecan Chicken

1 cup buttermilk*	250 ml
1 egg, beaten	
1 cup flour	120 g
1 cup very finely grated pecans	110 g
2 tablespoons sesame seeds	15 g
2 teaspoons paprika	10 ml
6 - 8 boneless, skinless, chicken breast halves	
¼ cup (½ stick) butter	60 g
½ cup chopped pecans	55 g

- Preheat oven to 350° (175° C).

- Combine buttermilk and egg in shallow bowl.

- In separate bowl, combine flour, grated pecans, sesame seeds, paprika, 1 teaspoon (5 ml) salt and ¼ teaspoon (1 ml) pepper.

- Dip chicken breasts in egg-milk mixture and coat well in flour-pecan mixture.

- Melt butter in large baking pan and place breaded chicken in pan. Sprinkle chopped pecans over chicken breasts.

- Bake for 30 to 35 minutes or until flour mixture is light brown. Serves 8.

TIP: To make buttermilk, mix 1 cup (250 ml) milk with 1 tablespoon (15 ml) lemon juice or vinegar and let milk rest for about 10 minutes.

Chicken Tarragon

*Tarragon works wonders
for this chicken.*

1 (8 ounce) package egg noodles	230 g
1 cup dry white wine	250 ml
1 teaspoon dried tarragon leaves	5 ml
1 (1 ounce) packet dry vegetable soup mix	30 g
4 boneless, skinless chicken breast halves	
1 (8 ounce) carton sour cream	230 g

- Cook noodles according to package directions, drain and set aside. Pour 2 cups (500 ml) water to large skillet. Over medium heat add wine and tarragon and bring to boil. Stir in dry soup mix and boil for 5 minutes.

- Add chicken and reduce heat. Cover and simmer for 15 minutes or until juices run clear. Arrange noodles on serving dish. Use slotted spoon to remove chicken, place on top of noodles and cover with foil.

- Boil juices in skillet for about 5 to 10 minutes or until liquid reduces to ½ cup (125 ml). Turn heat to low and stir constantly while adding sour cream. Heat for 3 to 4 minutes more and pour over chicken. Serves 4.

Q: Why can't a rooster ever get rich?

A: Because he works for chicken feed.

Slow Clucker

Pluck a little oregano here, stir in some veggies there, throw in some chicken and let your slow cooker do all the work! Over 60 savory chicken recipes allow you to add ingredients to the cooker, go about your busy day and come home to a warm, wonderful dinner surely to please your flock.

Slow Clucker Contents

Arroz con Pollo

3 pounds chicken thighs	1.3 kg
2 (15 ounce) cans Italian stewed tomatoes	2 (425 g)
1 (16 ounce) package frozen green peas, thawed	455 g
2 cups long grain rice	370 g
1 (.3 ounce) packet yellow rice seasoning mix	10 g
2 (14 ounce) cans chicken broth	2 (400 g)
1 heaping teaspoon minced garlic	5 ml
1 teaspoon dried oregano	5 ml

- Combine all ingredients plus ¾ cup (175 ml) water in sprayed slow cooker and stir well.

- Cover and cook on LOW for 7 to 8 hours or on HIGH for 3 hours 30 minutes to 4 hours. Serves 10.

Bacon-Wrapped Fiesta Chicken

1 (2.5 ounce) jar dried beef	70 g
6 boneless, skinless chicken breast halves	
6 slices bacon	
2 (10 ounce) cans golden mushroom soup	2 (280 g)
1 (6 ounce) package parmesan-butter rice, cooked	170 g

- Place dried beef sliced in 5-quart (5 L) slow cooker. Roll each chicken breast in slice of bacon and place over dried beef.

- Pour mushroom soup and ⅓ cup (75 ml) water in saucepan, heat just enough to mix and pour over chicken. Cover and cook on LOW for 7 to 8 hours. Serve over rice. Serves 6.

Artichoke-Chicken Pasta

1½ pounds boneless chicken breast tenders	680 g
1 (15 ounce) can artichoke hearts, quartered	425 g
¾ cup roasted red peppers, chopped	110 g
1 (8 ounce) package American cheese, shredded	230 g
1 tablespoon white wine Worcestershire sauce	15 ml
1 (10 ounce) can cream of chicken soup	280 g
1 (8 ounce) package shredded cheddar cheese	230 g
4 cups hot, cooked bow-tie pasta	300 g

- Combine chicken tenders, artichoke, roasted peppers, American cheese, Worcestershire sauce and soup in slow cooker and mix well.

- Cover and cook on LOW for 6 to 8 hours. About 20 minutes before serving, fold in cheddar cheese, hot pasta, and a little salt and pepper. Serves 8.

Cooked chicken should not be left out of the refrigerator longer than two hours.

Broccoli-Rice Chicken

1¼ cups rice	120 g
2 pounds boneless, skinless chicken breast halves	910 g
1 teaspoon dried parsley	5 ml
1 (1.8 ounce) packet cream of broccoli soup mix	45 g
1 (14 ounce) can chicken broth	400 g

- Place rice in lightly sprayed slow cooker. Cut chicken into slices and put over rice.

- Sprinkle with parsley.

- Combine soup mix, chicken broth and 1 cup (250 ml) water in saucepan. Heat just enough to mix well. Pour over chicken and rice.

- Cover and cook on LOW for 6 to 8 hours. Serves 8.

Stuffy Chicken

This is a great recipe for leftover chicken.

1 (10 ounce) can cream of chicken soup	280 g
2 ribs celery, sliced	
½ cup (1 stick) butter, melted	115 g
3 cups cooked cubed chicken	420 g
1 (16 ounce) package frozen broccoli, corn and bell peppers	455 g
1 (8 ounce) box cornbread stuffing mix	230 g

- Combine chicken soup, celery, butter, cubed chicken, vegetables, stuffing mix and ⅓ cup (75 ml) water in large saucepan and heat just enough to mix well.

- Transfer to sprayed 5 to 6-quart (5 to 6 L) slow cooker. Cover and cook on LOW for 5 to 6 hours. Serves 8.

Chicken Alfredo

1½ pounds boneless chicken thighs	680 g
2 ribs celery, sliced diagonally	
1 red bell pepper, julienned	
1 (16 ounce) jar alfredo sauce	455 g
3 cups fresh broccoli florets	215 g
1 (8 ounce) package fettuccini or linguine	230 g
1 (5 ounce) package grated parmesan cheese	145 g

- Cut chicken into strips. Layer chicken, celery and bell pepper in 4 to 5-quart (4 to 5 L) slow cooker. Pour alfredo sauce evenly over vegetables. Cover and cook on LOW for 5 to 6 hours.

- About 30 minutes before serving, turn heat to HIGH and add broccoli florets to chicken-alfredo mixture. Cover and cook for an additional 30 minutes. Serves 8.

- Cook pasta according to package directions and drain. Just before serving pour pasta into cooker, mix and sprinkle parmesan cheese on top.

Chicken Meets Italy

1 (16 ounce) package frozen whole green beans, thawed	455 g
1 onion, chopped	
1 cup halved fresh mushrooms	70 g
3 boneless, skinless chicken breast halves	
1 (15 ounce) can Italian stewed tomatoes	425 g
1 teaspoon chicken bouillon granules	5 ml
1 teaspoon minced garlic	5 ml
1 teaspoon Italian seasoning	5 ml
1 (8 ounce) package fettuccini	230 g
1 (4 ounce) package parmesan cheese	145 g

- Place green beans, onion and mushrooms in sprayed 4 to 5-quart (4 to 5 L) slow cooker. Cut chicken into 1-inch (2.5 cm) pieces and place over vegetables.

- Combine stewed tomatoes, chicken bouillon, garlic and Italian seasoning in small bowl. Pour over chicken. Cover and cook on LOW for 5 to 6 hours.

- Cook fettuccini according to package directions and drain. Serve chicken over fettuccini and sprinkle with parmesan cheese. Serves 6.

TIP: For added flavor, you can add ¼ cup (60 g) butter.

Chicken and Everything Good

2 (10 ounce) cans cream
   of chicken soup   2 (280 g)
⅓ cup (⅔ stick) butter,
   melted   75 g
3 cups cooked, cubed
   chicken   420 g
1 (16 ounce) package
   frozen broccoli,
   corn, red peppers   455 g
1 (10 ounce) package
   frozen green peas   280 g
1 (8 ounce) package
   cornbread stuffing
   mix   230 g

- Combine soup, melted butter and ⅓ cup (75 ml) water in large saucepan, heat just enough to mix well.

- Add chicken, vegetables and stuffing mix and stir well. Spoon mixture into sprayed slow cooker. Cover and cook on LOW for 5 to 6 hours or on HIGH for 3 hours. Serves 8.

Chicken-in-the-Garden

4 - 5 boneless, skinless
   chicken breast halves
1 (16 ounce) package frozen
   broccoli, cauliflower and
   carrots, thawed   455 g
1 (10 ounce) can cream of
   celery soup   280 g
1 (8 ounce) package
   shredded cheddar- Jack
   cheese, divided   230 g

- Cut chicken into strips and place chicken strips sprinkled with 2 teaspoons (10 ml) salt in sprayed slow cooker.

- Combine vegetables, celery soup and half cheese in saucepan and heat just enough to mix well. Spoon over chicken breasts.

- Cover and cook on LOW for 4 to 5 hours. About 10 minutes before serving, sprinkle remaining cheese on top of casserole. Serves 6.

Chicken Curry Over Rice

3 boneless, skinless chicken
   breast halves
½ cup chicken broth   125 ml
1 (10 ounce) can cream of
   chicken soup   280 g
1 onion, coarsely chopped
1 red bell pepper, cut into
   strips
¼ cup golden raisins   40 g
1½ teaspoons curry powder   7 ml
¼ teaspoon ground ginger   1 ml
Rice, cooked

- Cut chicken into thin strips.

- Combine chicken strips, broth, soup, onion, bell pepper, raisins, curry powder and ginger in saucepan just enough to mix well.

- Pour into sprayed 5 to 6-quart (5 to 6 L) slow cooker, cover and cook on LOW for 3 to 4 hours. Serve over rice. Serves 4.

Chicken Sherry

5 - 6 boneless skinless chicken
   breast halves
1 (16 ounce) package frozen
   broccoli florets, thawed   455 g
1 red bell pepper, julienne
1 (16 ounce) jar Ragu®
   parmesan-mozzarella
   cheese creation sauce   455 g
3 tablespoons sherry   45 ml
Noodles, cooked

- Brown chicken breasts in skillet and place in sprayed oval 5 to 6-quart (5 to 6 L) slow cooker.

- Place broccoli florets on plate, remove stems and discard.

- Combine broccoli florets, bell pepper, cheese sauce and sherry in bowl and mix well. Spoon over chicken breasts.

- Cover and cook on LOW for 4 to 5 hours. Serve over buttered noodles. Serves 6.

Chicken Breast Deluxe

4 slices bacon
5 - 6 boneless, skinless
   chicken breast halves
1 cup sliced celery   100 g
1 cup sliced red bell pepper   150 g
1 (10 ounce) can cream of
   chicken soup   280 g
2 tablespoons white wine or
   cooking wine   30 ml
6 slices Swiss cheese
2 tablespoons dried parsley   30 ml

- Cook bacon in large skillet, drain, crumble and set aside drippings.

- Place chicken in skillet with bacon drippings and lightly brown on both sides.

- Transfer chicken to sprayed slow cooker and place celery and red bell pepper over chicken.

- In same skillet, combine soup and wine, heat just enough to mix well and spoon over vegetables and chicken in slow cooker. Cover and cook on LOW for 3 to 4 hours.

- Top with slices of cheese over each chicken breast, sprinkle with parsley and cook for an additional 10 minutes.

- When serving, sprinkle crumbled bacon over each serving. Serves 6.

Chicken Coq au Vin

4 chicken quarters
Olive oil
10 - 12 small white onions,
    peeled
½ pound whole button
    mushrooms   230 g
1 teaspoon minced garlic   5 ml
½ teaspoon dried thyme
    leaves   2 ml
10 - 12 small new
    (red) potatoes with peels
1 (10 ounce) can chicken
    broth   280 g
1 cup burgundy wine   250 ml
6 bacon slices, cooked,
    crumbled

- Brown chicken quarters in skillet with oil on both sides and set aside.

- Place white onions, whole mushrooms, garlic and thyme in oblong slow cooker.

- Add chicken quarters, potatoes, chicken broth and a little salt and pepper.

- Cover and cook on LOW for 8 to 10 hours or on HIGH for 3 to 4 hours.

- During last hour, turn heat to HIGH, add burgundy and continue cooking.

- Sprinkle crumbled bacon over chicken before serving. Serves 4 to 6.

Veggie-Chicken for Supper

5 - 6 boneless, skinless
  chicken breasts halves
6 carrots, cut in (1 inch)
  lengths   **2.5 cm**
1 (15 ounce) can cut
  green beans,
  drained   **425 g**
1 (15 ounce) can whole
  new potatoes,
  drained   **425 g**
2 (10 ounce) cans cream
  of mushroom soup   2 (280 g)
Shredded cheddar cheese

- Wash, dry chicken breasts with paper towels and place in sprayed oblong slow cooker.

- Combine, carrots, green beans, potatoes and mushroom soup in saucepan, heat just enough to mix well and pour over chicken in cooker.

- Cover and cook on LOW for 8 to 10 hours. When ready to serve, sprinkle cheese on top. Serves 6.

Q: Which side of a chicken has the most feathers?

A: The outside.

Chicken-Celery Delight

¾ cup cooked white rice   120 g

1 (14 ounce) can
    chicken broth   400 g

1 (1 ounce) packet onion
    soup mix   30 g

1 red bell pepper,
    seeded, chopped

2 (10 ounce) cans cream
    of celery soup   2 (280 g)

¾ cup white cooking
    wine   175 ml

4 - 6 boneless, skinless
    chicken breasts halves

1 (5 ounce) package
    grated parmesan
    cheese   145 g

- Combine rice, broth, soup mix, bell pepper, celery soup, ¾ cup (175 ml) water, wine and several sprinkles of black pepper in saucepan and heat just enough to mix well.

- Place chicken breasts in sprayed 6-quart (6 L) oval slow cooker. Pour rice-soup mixture over chicken breasts. Cover and cook on LOW for 4 to 6 hours.

- One hour before serving, sprinkle parmesan cheese over chicken. Serves 6.

Whole Lotta Chicken Dinner

1 cup rice	95 g
1 tablespoon chicken seasoning	15 ml
1 (1 ounce) packet onion soup mix	30 g
1 green bell pepper, seeded, chopped	
1 (4 ounce) jar diced pimentos, drained well	115 g
¾ teaspoon dried basil	4 ml
1 (14 ounce) can chicken broth	400 g
1 (10 ounce) can cream of chicken soup	280 g
5 - 6 boneless, skinless chicken breast halves	

- Combine rice, chicken seasoning, onion soup mix, bell pepper, pimentos, basil, broth, ½ cup (125 ml) water and chicken soup in saucepan and heat just enough to mix well.

- Place chicken breasts in sprayed slow cooker and cover chicken with rice mixture. Cover and cook on LOW for 6 to 7 hours. Serves 6.

Q: Why couldn't the chicken find her eggs?

A: Because she mislaid them.

Chicken for the Gods

1¾ cups flour	210 g
2 tablespoons dry mustard	30 ml
6 boneless, skinless chicken breast halves	
2 tablespoons olive oil	30 ml
1 (10 ounce) can chicken and rice soup	280 g

- Place flour and mustard in shallow bowl and dredge chicken breasts.

- Brown chicken breasts in skillet with oil. Place all breasts in sprayed 6-quart (6 L) oval slow cooker.

- Pour chicken and rice soup over chicken and add about ¼ (60 ml) cup water.

- Cover and cook on LOW for 6 to 7 hours. Serves 6.

Stuffed Chicken-Ready Supper

1 (6 ounce) package chicken stuffing mix	170 g
3 cups cooked, chopped chicken breast halves	420 g
1 (16 ounce) package frozen whole green beans, thawed	455 g
2 (12 ounce) jars chicken gravy	2 (340 g)

- Prepare stuffing mix according to package directions and place in sprayed, oval slow cooker.

- Follow with layer of chopped chicken or leftover turkey breasts and place green beans over chicken. Pour chicken gravy over green beans.

- Cover and cook on LOW for 3 hours 30 minutes to 4 hours 30 minutes. Serves 8.

Cream Cheese Chicken

4 boneless, skinless chicken
    breast halves
2 tablespoons butter, melted   30 g
1 (10 ounce) can cream of
    mushroom soup   280 g
1 (.4 ounce) packet Italian
    salad dressing mix   10 g
½ cup sherry   125 ml
1 (8 ounce) package cream
    cheese, cubed   230 g
Noodles, cooked

- Wash chicken breasts, dry with paper towels, brush melted butter over chicken and place in sprayed slow cooker. Add remaining ingredients to saucepan, heat just enough to mix well and add to slow cooker.

- Cover and cook on LOW for 6 to 7 hours. Serve over hot, buttered noodles. Serves 4.

Creamy Chicken and Potatoes

4 boneless, skinless chicken
    breast halves
2 teaspoons chicken
    seasoning   10 ml
8 - 10 small new (red)
    potatoes with peels
1 (10 ounce) can cream of
    chicken soup   280 g
1 (8 ounce) carton sour
    cream   230 g

- Place chicken breast halves, sprinkled with chicken seasoning in slow cooker. Arrange new potatoes around chicken.

- Combine soup, sour cream and lots of pepper in saucepan and heat just enough to mix well. Spoon over chicken breast. Cover and cook on LOW for 4 to 6 hours. Serves 4.

Happy Hearty Chicken

4 - 5 carrots, peeled
6 medium new (red) potatoes
   with peels, quartered
4 - 5 boneless, skinless
   chicken breast halves
1 tablespoon chicken
   seasoning   **15 ml**
2 (10 ounce) cans cream
   of chicken soup   **2 (280 g)**
⅓ cup white wine or
   cooking wine   **75 ml**

- Cut carrots into ½-inch (1.2 cm) pieces. Place potatoes and carrots in slow cooker. Sprinkle chicken breasts with chicken seasoning and place over vegetables.

- Heat soups with ¼ cup (60 ml) water and wine in saucepan, heat just enough to mix well and pour over chicken and vegetables. Cover and cook on LOW for 5 to 6 hours. Serves 5.

TIP: *For a tasty change, use 1 (10 ounce/280 g) can chicken soup and 1 (10 ounce/280 g) can mushroom soup instead of cream of chicken soup.*

Q: What do you get when you cross a chicken with gum?

A: Chicklets.

Chicken with Orange Sauce

1 whole chicken, quartered
½ cup plus 2 tablespoons
    flour   110 g
½ teaspoon ground nutmeg   2 ml
½ teaspoon ground
    cinnamon   2 ml
2 large sweet potatoes,
    peeled, sliced
1 (8 ounce) can pineapple
    chunks with juice   230 g
1 (10 ounce) can cream of
    chicken soup   280 g
⅔ cup orange juice   150 ml
Rice, cooked

- Wash and dry chicken quarters with paper towels. Combine ½ cup (60 g) flour, nutmeg and cinnamon in bowl and coat chicken. Place sweet potatoes and pineapple in large sprayed slow cooker. Arrange chicken on top.

- Combine chicken soup, orange juice and remaining flour in saucepan, heat just enough to mix well and pour over chicken. Cover and cook on LOW for 7 to 9 hours or on HIGH for 3 to 4 hours. Serve over hot, buttered rice. Serves 6.

Chow Mein Chicken

4 boneless, skinless chicken
    breast halves
2 - 3 cups sliced celery
1 onion, coarsely chopped
¼ cup soy sauce   **60 ml**
¼ teaspoon cayenne pepper
1 (14 ounce) can chicken
    broth   **400 g**
1 (15 ounce) can bean
    sprouts, drained   **425 g**
1 (8 ounce) can water
    chestnuts, drained   **230 g**
1 (15 ounce) can bamboo
    shoots   **425 g**
¼ cup flour   **30 g**
1 (6 ounce) package chow
    mein noodles   **170 g**

- Combine chicken, celery, onion, soy sauce, cayenne pepper and chicken broth in sprayed slow cooker. Cover and cook on LOW for 3 to 4 hours.

- Add bean sprouts, water chestnuts and bamboo shoots to chicken.

- Mix flour and ¼ cup (60 ml) water and stir into chicken and vegetables. Cook an additional 1 hour.

- Serve over chow mein noodles. Serves 4.

Creamed Chicken and Vegetables

1 (10 ounce) can cream of
    chicken soup   **280 g**
4 large boneless, skinless
    chicken breast halves,
    sliced thinly
1 (16 ounce) package frozen
    peas and carrots,
    thawed   **455 g**
1 (12 ounce) jar chicken
    gravy   **340 g**

- Pour soup and ½ cup (125 ml) water into sprayed 6-quart (6 L) slow cooker.

- Mix and add chicken slices. Sprinkle a little salt and lots of pepper over chicken and soup.

- Cover and cook on LOW for 4 to 5 hours.

- Add peas and carrots, chicken gravy and ½ cup (125 ml) water. Increase heat to HIGH and cook for about 1 hour or until peas and carrots are tender. Serves 6.

TIP: *Serve over large, refrigerated buttermilk biscuits or over thick Texas toast.*

The record for laying the most eggs in a day is seven eggs.

Creamed Chicken

**4 large boneless, skinless
    chicken breast halves**
Lemon juice
1 red bell pepper, chopped
2 ribs celery, sliced diagonally
**1 (10 ounce) can cream of
    chicken soup**   **280 g**
**1 (10 ounce) can cream of
    celery soup**   **280 g**
⅓ cup dry white wine   **75 ml**
**1 (5 ounce) package grated
    parmesan cheese**   **145 g**
Rice, cooked

- Wash and pat chicken dry with paper towels, rub a little lemon juice over chicken and sprinkle with salt and pepper. Place in slow cooker and top with bell pepper and celery.

- Combine soups and wine in saucepan and heat just enough to mix thoroughly. Pour over chicken breasts and sprinkle with parmesan cheese.

- Cover and cook on LOW for 6 to 7 hours. Serve over buttered rice. Serves 4.

Creamy Salsa Chicken

**4 - 5 boneless, skinless
  chicken breast halves**
**1 (1 ounce) packet taco
  seasoning mix** .... **30 g**
1 cup salsa .... **265 g**
½ cup sour cream .... **240 g**

- Place chicken breasts in 5 to 6-quart (5 to 6 L) oval slow cooker and add ¼ cup (60 ml) water.

- Sprinkle taco seasoning mix over chicken and top with salsa. Cook on LOW for 5 to 6 hours.

- When ready to serve, remove chicken breasts and place on platter. Stir sour cream into juices and spoon over chicken breasts. Serves 5.

Delightful Chicken and Veggies

**4 - 5 boneless skinless,
  chicken breast halves**
**1 (15 ounce) can whole
  kernel corn, drained** ...... **425 g**
**1 (10 ounce) box frozen
  green peas, thawed** .... **280 g**
**1 (16 ounce) jar alfredo
  sauce** .... **455 g**
**1 teaspoon chicken
  seasoning** .... **5 ml**
1 teaspoon minced garlic .. **5 ml**
Pasta, cooked

- Brown chicken breasts in skillet and place in sprayed oval slow cooker.

- Combine corn, peas, alfredo sauce, ¼ cup (60 ml) water, chicken seasoning and minced garlic in bowl and pour over chicken breasts.

- Cover and cook on LOW for 4 to 5 hours. Serve over pasta. Serves 5.

Delicious Chicken Pasta

1 pound chicken tenders	**455 g**
Lemon-herb chicken seasoning	
3 tablespoons butter	**35 g**
1 onion, coarsely chopped	
1 (15 ounce) can diced tomatoes	**425 g**
1 (10 ounce) can golden mushroom soup	**280 g**
1 (8 ounce) box angel hair pasta	**230 g**

- Pat chicken tenders dry with several paper towels and sprinkle ample amount of chicken seasoning.

- Melt butter in large skillet, brown chicken and place in oval slow cooker. Pour remaining butter over chicken and cover with onion.

- In separate bowl, combine diced tomatoes and mushroom soup and pour over chicken and onions. Cover and cook on LOW for 4 to 5 hours.

- When ready to serve, cook pasta according to package directions. Serve chicken and sauce over pasta. Serves 8.

Easy Slow-Cooked Chicken

5 boneless, skinless chicken
   breast halves
2 (10 ounce) cans cream
   of chicken soup   **2 (280 g)**
1 (6 ounce) box chicken
   stuffing mix   **170 g**
1 (16 ounce) package
   frozen green peas,
   thawed   **455 g**

- Place chicken breasts in 6-quart (6 L) slow cooker and spoon soups over chicken.

- Combine stuffing mix with ingredients according to package directions; include seasoning packet in bowl and spoon over chicken and soup.

- Cover and cook on LOW for 5 to 6 hours.

- Sprinkle drained green peas over top of stuffing. Cover and cook for an additional 45 to 50 minutes. Serves 5.

The greatest number of yolks in one chicken egg is nine.

Farmhouse Supper

1 (8 ounce) package medium noodles	230 g
4 - 5 boneless, skinless chicken breast halves	
1 (14 ounce) can chicken broth	400 g
2 cups sliced celery	200 g
2 onions, chopped	
1 green bell pepper, seeded, chopped	
1 red bell pepper, seeded, chopped	
1 (10 ounce) can cream of chicken soup	280 g
1 (10 ounce) can cream of mushroom soup	280 g
1 cup shredded 4-cheese blend	115 g

- Cook noodles in boiling water until barely tender and drain well. Cut chicken into thin slices.

- Combine noodles, chicken and broth in large, sprayed slow cooker and mix. (Make sure noodles separate and coat with broth.)

- Combine remaining ingredients in saucepan and heat just enough to mix well and add to slow cooker. Cover and cook on LOW for 4 to 6 hours. Serves 5.

Golden Chicken Dinner

5 boneless, skinless chicken
   breast halves
6 medium new (red) potatoes
   with peels, cubed
6 medium carrots, peeled,
   quartered
1 tablespoon dried parsley
   flakes   15 ml
1 (10 ounce) can golden
   mushroom soup   280 g
1 (10 ounce) can cream of
   chicken soup   280 g
4 tablespoons dried mashed
   potato flakes   15 g

- Cut chicken into ½-inch (1.2 cm) pieces.

- Place potatoes and carrots in slow cooker and top with chicken breasts. Sprinkle parsley flakes, 1 teaspoon (5 ml) salt and a little pepper over chicken.

- Mix soups in bowl and spread over chicken. Cover and slow cook on LOW for 6 to 7 hours.

- Combine potato flakes and a little water or milk in bowl, mix to make gravy and cook for additional 30 minutes. Serves 8.

Imperial Chicken

1 (6 ounce) box long
    grain-wild rice   170 g
1 (16 ounce) jar roasted
    garlic-parmesan
    cheese creation   455 g
6 boneless, skinless chicken
    breast halves
1 (16 ounce) package frozen
    French-style green
    beans, thawed   455 g
½ cup slivered almonds,
    toasted   85 g

- Pour 2½ cups (625 ml) water, rice and seasoning packet into sprayed oval slow cooker and stir well.

- Spoon in cheese and mix well. Place chicken breasts in slow cooker and cover with green beans. Cover and cook on LOW for 3 to 5 hours.

- When ready to serve, sprinkle with slivered almonds. Serves 6.

Orange Russian Chicken

6 boneless, skinless chicken
    breasts halves
1½ cups orange marmalade   480 g
1 (8 ounce) bottle Russian
    salad dressing   250 ml
1 (1 ounce) packet onion
    soup mix   30 g

- Place chicken breasts in oval slow cooker. Combine orange marmalade, salad dressing, soup mix and ¾ cup (175 ml) water in bowl and stir well.

- Spoon mixture over chicken breasts. Cover and cook on LOW for 4 to 6 hours. Serves 6.

Italian Chicken

1 small head cabbage
1 onion
1 (4 ounce) jar sliced
    mushrooms,
    drained   115 g
1 medium zucchini,
    sliced
1 red bell pepper,
    julienned
1 teaspoon Italian
    seasoning   5 ml
1½ pounds skinless
    chicken thighs   680 g
1 teaspoon minced
    garlic   5 ml
2 (15 ounce) cans Italian
    stewed tomatoes 2 (425 g)

- Cut cabbage into wedges, slice onions and separate into rings. Make layers of cabbage, onion, mushrooms, zucchini and bell pepper in sprayed 6-quart (6 L) slow cooker.

- Sprinkle Italian seasoning over vegetables. Place chicken thighs on top of vegetables.

- Mix garlic with tomatoes in bowl and pour over chicken. Cover and cook on LOW for 4 to 6 hours. Serves 6.

TIP: *When serving, sprinkle a little parmesan cheese over each serving.*

Q: What do you get if you cross a chicken with a bell?

A: A bird that has to ring its own neck.

Mushroom Chicken

4 boneless, skinless
chicken breast halves
1 (15 ounce) can tomato
sauce   425 g
2 (4 ounce) cans sliced
mushrooms,
drained   2 (115 g)
1 (10 ounce) package
frozen seasoning
blend onions
and peppers,
thawed   280 g
2 teaspoons Italian
seasoning   10 ml
1 teaspoon minced
garlic   5 ml

- Brown chicken breasts in skillet and place in sprayed oval slow cooker.

- Combine tomato sauce, mushrooms, onions and peppers, Italian seasoning, minced garlic and ¼ cup (60 ml) water in bowl and spoon over chicken breasts.

- Cover and cook on LOW for 4 to 5 hours. Serves 4.

Diner: Do you serve chicken here?

Waiter: Sit down, sir. We serve anyone.

Quick-Fix Chicken

4 - 6 boneless, skinless
   chicken breast halves
1 (8 ounce) carton sour
   cream   230 g
¼ cup soy sauce   60 ml
2 (10 ounce) cans
   French onion soup   2 (280 g)

- Wash and dry chicken with paper towels and place in sprayed oval slow cooker.

- Combine sour cream, soy sauce and onion soup in bowl, stir and mix well. Pour over chicken.

- Cover and cook on LOW for 5 to 6 hours if chicken breasts are large, 3 to 4 hours if breasts are medium. Serves 6.

TIP: *Serve chicken and sauce with hot, buttered rice or mashed potatoes.*

Perfect Chicken Breasts

1 (2.5 ounce) jar dried
   beef   70 g
6 small boneless,
   skinless chicken
   breast halves
6 slices bacon
2 (10 ounce) cans golden
   mushroom soup   2 (280 g)

- Line bottom of oval slow cooker with slices of dried beef and overlap some.

- Roll each chicken breast with slice of bacon and secure with toothpick. Place in slow cooker, overlapping as little as possible.

- Combine mushroom soup and ½ cup (125 ml) water or milk in saucepan, heat just enough to mix well and spoon over chicken breasts.

- Cover and cook on LOW for 6 to 8 hours. Serves 6.

TIP: *When cooked, you will have a great "gravy" that is wonderful served over noodles or rice.*

Russian Chicken

1 (8 ounce) bottle Russian
salad dressing .... 250 ml
1 (16 ounce) can whole
cranberry sauce .... 455 g
1 (1 ounce) packet onion
soup mix .... 30 g
1 whole chicken, skinned,
quartered
Rice, cooked

• Combine dressing, cranberry sauce, ½ cup (125 ml) water and soup mix in bowl. Stir well. Place chicken pieces in 6-quart (6 L) oval slow cooker and spoon dressing-cranberry mixture over chicken.

• Cover and cook on LOW for 4 to 5 hours. Serve sauce and chicken over rice. Serve 4 to 6.

TIP: *If you don't want to cut up a chicken, use 6 chicken breasts.*

Chicken Noodle Delight

5 - 6 boneless, skinless
chicken breast halves
1 teaspoon chicken
seasoning .... 5 ml
1 (10 ounce) can cream of
chicken soup .... 280 g
1 (10 ounce) can
broccoli-cheese soup ... 280 g
½ cup white cooking wine ... 125 ml
1 (12 ounce) package
medium noodles,
cooked .... 340 g

• Cut chicken breasts in half if they are unusually large. Place breast halves, sprinkled with pepper and chicken seasoning in sprayed slow cooker.

• Combine soups and wine in saucepan and heat enough to mix well. Pour over chicken.

• Cover and cook on LOW for 5 to 6 hours. Serve chicken and sauce over noodles. Serves 6.

Saffron Rice and Chicken

1 fryer-broiler chicken,
    quartered
½ teaspoon garlic powder   2 ml
Olive oil
1 (14 ounce) can chicken
    broth   400 g
1 onion, chopped
1 green bell pepper, seeded,
    chopped
1 yellow bell pepper, seeded,
    chopped
1 (4 ounce) jar pimentos,
    drained   115 g
⅓ cup bacon bits   40 g
1 (5 ounce) package saffron
    yellow rice mix   145 g
2 tablespoons (¼ stick)
    butter, melted   30 g

- Sprinkle chicken with garlic powder and a little salt and pepper. Brown chicken quarters in skillet with a little oil. Place chicken in sprayed oval slow cooker and pour broth in slow cooker.

- Combine, onion, bell peppers, pimentos and bacon bits in bowl and spoon over chicken quarters. Cover and cook on LOW for 4 to 5 hours.

- Carefully remove chicken quarters from cooker, stir in rice mix and butter and return chicken to cooker. Cover and cook for 1 hour or until rice is tender. Serves 4 to 6.

Savory Chicken Fettuccini

2 pounds boneless, skinless
   chicken thighs, cubed   1 kg
½ teaspoon garlic powder   2 ml
1 red bell pepper, seeded,
   chopped
2 ribs celery, chopped
1 (10 ounce) can cream of
   celery soup   280 g
1 (10 ounce) can cream of
   chicken soup   280 g
1 (8 ounce) package cubed
   Velveeta® cheese   227 g
1 (4 ounce) jar diced
   pimentos   114 g
1 (16 ounce) package spinach
   fettuccini   454 g

- Place chicken in sprayed slow cooker. Sprinkle with garlic powder, ½ teaspoon (2 ml) pepper, bell pepper and celery. Mix soups (no water) in bowl and pour on chicken.

- Cover and cook on HIGH for 4 to 6 hours or until chicken juices are clear. Stir in cheese and pimentos. Cover and cook until cheese melts.

- Cook fettuccini according to package directions and drain. Place fettuccini in serving bowl and spoon chicken over fettuccini. Serve hot.

Slow-Cook Arroz con Pollo

This is a classic Southwest chicken and rice dinner, but cooked conveniently in a slow cooker.

3 - 4 pounds boneless, skinless chicken breasts and thighs
1 (15 ounce) can Mexican-stewed tomatoes   425 g
1½ cups long grain rice   280 g
1 (3 ounce) package yellow rice with seasoning mix   85 g
2 (14 ounce) cans chicken broth   2 (400 g)
1 clove garlic, minced
1 teaspoon oregano   5 ml
1 teaspoon chili powder   5 ml

• Combine all ingredients plus ¾ cup (175 ml) water in large, sprayed slow cooker and stir well.

• Cover and cook on LOW for 7 to 8 hours or on HIGH for 3 hours 30 minutes to 4 hours. Serves 10 to 12.

Slow-Cooker Cordon Bleu

4 boneless, skinless chicken breast halves
4 slices cooked ham
4 slices Swiss cheese, softened
1 (10 ounce) can cream of chicken soup   280 g
¼ cup milk   60 ml
Noodles, cooked

• Place chicken breasts on cutting board and pound until breast halves are thin. Place ham and cheese slices on chicken breasts, roll and secure with toothpick.

• Arrange chicken rolls in 4-quart (4 L) slow cooker. Thin chicken soup with milk in saucepan and heat just enough to mix well and pour over chicken rolls.

• Cover and cook on LOW for 4 to 5 hours. Serve over noodles and cover with sauce from soup. Serves 4.

Slow-Cook Chicken Fajitas

This is a convenient way to have a popular one-pot dinner.

2 pounds boneless, skinless chicken breast halves	**910 g**
1 onion, thinly sliced	
1 red bell pepper, seeded, sliced	
1 teaspoon ground cumin	**5 ml**
1½ teaspoons chili powder	**7 ml**
1 tablespoon lime juice	**15 ml**
½ cup chicken broth	**125 ml**
8 - 10 warmed flour tortillas	
Guacamole	
Sour cream	
Lettuce	
Tomatoes	

- Cut chicken into diagonal strips and place in sprayed slow cooker. Top with onion and bell pepper.

- Combine cumin, chili powder, lime juice and chicken broth in bowl and pour over chicken and vegetables. Cover and cook on LOW for 5 to 7 hours.

- When serving, spoon several slices of chicken mixture with sauce into center of each warm tortilla and fold. Serve with guacamole, sour cream, lettuce and/or tomatoes. Serves 8.

Chicken Little Slow-Cook

**4 boneless, skinless chicken
    breast halves**
**1 (10 ounce) can French
    onion soup**   **280 g**
**2 teaspoons chicken
    seasoning**   **10 ml**
**1 (4 ounce) jar sliced
    mushrooms, drained**   **115 g**
**1 cup shredded mozzarella
    cheese**   **115 g**

- Brown each chicken breast in skillet and place in oval slow cooker.

- Pour onion soup over chicken and sprinkle pepper and chicken seasoning over chicken breasts.

- Place mushrooms and cheese over chicken breasts. Cover and cook on LOW for 4 to 5 hours. Serves 4.

TIP: To make this chicken really festive when ready to serve, sprinkle some chopped green onions over each serving.

The term "feathered out" is used when a chick loses its cute fuzz and grows its feathers.

So-Good Chicken

4 - 5 boneless, skinless
   chicken breast halves
1 (10 ounce) can golden
   mushroom soup   280 g
1 cup white cooking wine   250 ml
1 (8 ounce) carton sour
   cream   230 g

- Wash and dry chicken breasts with paper towels and sprinkle a little salt and pepper over each and place in slow cooker.

- Combine mushroom soup, wine and sour cream in saucepan and heat just enough to mix well. Spoon over chicken breasts. Cover and cook on LOW for 5 to 7 hours. Serves 5.

Lemon Chicken

1 (2½ - 3 pound)
   chicken, quartered   1.1 - 1.4 kg
1 teaspoon dried
   oregano   5 ml
2 teaspoons minced
   garlic   10 ml
2 tablespoons butter   30 g
¼ cup lemon juice   60 ml

- Season chicken quarters with salt, pepper and oregano and rub garlic on chicken.

- Brown chicken quarters on all sides in butter in skillet and transfer to sprayed oval slow cooker.

- Add ⅓ cup (75 ml) water to skillet, scrape bottom and pour over chicken.

- Cover and cook on LOW for 5 to 7 hours.

- Pour lemon juice over chicken and cook for an additional 1 hour. Serves 6.

Southern Chicken

1 cup half-and-half cream	250 ml
1 tablespoon flour	15 ml
1 (1 ounce) packet chicken gravy mix	30 g
1 pound boneless, skinless chicken thighs	455 g
1 (16 ounce) package frozen stew vegetables, thawed	455 g
1 (4 ounce) jar sliced mushrooms, drained	115 g
1 (10 ounce) package frozen green peas, thawed	280 g
1½ cups biscuit mix	180 g
1 bunch fresh green onions, chopped	
½ cup milk	125 ml

- Combine half-and-half cream, flour, gravy mix and 1 cup (250 ml) water in bowl, stir until smooth and pour in large slow cooker.

- Cut chicken into 1-inch (2.5 cm) pieces and add to slow cooker. Stir in stew vegetables and mushrooms.

- Cover and cook on LOW for 4 to 6 hours or until chicken is tender and sauce thickens. Stir in peas.

- Combine biscuit mix, onions and milk in bowl and mix well. Drop tablespoonfuls of dough onto chicken mixture.

- Change heat to HIGH, cover and cook for an additional 50 to 60 minutes. Serves 8.

Southwestern Chicken Pot

6 boneless, skinless chicken breast halves	
1 teaspoon ground cumin	5 ml
1 teaspoon chili powder	5 ml
1 (10 ounce) can cream of chicken soup	280 g
1 (10 ounce) can fiesta nacho cheese soup	280 g
1 cup salsa	265 g
Rice, cooked	
Floured tortillas	

- Place chicken breasts in sprayed, oval slow cooker sprinkled with cumin, chili powder and some salt and pepper.

- Combine soups and salsa in saucepan. Heat just enough to mix and pour over chicken breasts.

- Cover and cook on LOW for 6 to 7 hours. Serve over rice with warmed flour tortillas spread with butter. Serves 6.

Sweet-and-Spicy Chicken

2 pounds chicken thighs	910 g
¾ cup chili sauce	205 g
¾ cup packed brown sugar	165 g
1 (1 ounce) packet onion soup mix	30 g
⅛ teaspoon cayenne pepper	.5 ml
Rice, cooked	

- Arrange chicken pieces in bottom of sprayed 5-quart (5 L) slow cooker.

- Combine chili sauce, brown sugar, onion soup mix, cayenne pepper and ¼ cup (60 ml) water in bowl and spoon over chicken

- Cover and cook on LOW for 6 to 7 hours. Serve over rice. Serves 6.

Slow-Cook Taco Chicken

3 cups cooked, chopped chicken	420 g
1 (1 ounce) packet taco seasoning	30 g
1 cup white rice	185 g
2 cups chopped celery	200 g
1 green bell pepper, seeded, chopped	
2 (15 ounce) cans Mexican stewed tomatoes	2 (425 g)

- Combine chicken, taco seasoning, rice, celery, bell pepper and stewed tomatoes in bowl and mix well.

- Pour into 5-quart (5 L) slow cooker. Cover and cook on LOW for 3 to 4 hours. Serves 8.

TIP: *This is a great recipe for leftover chicken.*

Tangy Chicken Legs

12 - 15 chicken legs	
⅓ cup soy sauce	75 ml
⅔ cup packed brown sugar	150 g
⅛ teaspoon ground ginger	.5 ml

- Place chicken legs in 5-quart (5 L) slow cooker.

- Combine soy sauce, brown sugar, ¼ cup (60 ml) water and ginger in bowl and spoon over chicken legs.

- Cover and cook on LOW for 4 to 5 hours. Serves 6.

Tasty Chicken-Rice and Veggies

4 boneless, skinless chicken
    breast halves
2 (10 ounce) jars
    sweet-and-sour
    sauce   2 (280 g)
1 (16 ounce) package
    frozen broccoli,
    cauliflower and
    carrots, thawed   455 g
1 (10 ounce) package
    frozen baby peas,
    thawed   280 g
2 cups sliced celery   200 g
1 (6 ounce) package
    parmesan-butter
    rice mix   170 g
⅓ cup slivered almonds,
    toasted   55 g
Rice, cooked

- Cut chicken in 1-inch (2.5 cm) strips.

- Combine chicken, sweet-and-sour sauce and all vegetables in 6-quart (6 L) sprayed slow cooker. Cover and cook on LOW for 4 to 6 hours.

- When ready to serve cook parmesan-butter rice according to package directions and fold in almonds.

- Serve chicken and vegetables over rice. Serves 4.

Tortilla Flats Chicken Bake

6 (6 inch) corn tortillas,
    divided   6 (15 cm)
3 cups cooked, cubed
    chicken   420 g
1 (10 ounce) package
    frozen corn   280 g
1 (15 ounce) can pinto
    beans with juice   425 g
1 (16 ounce) hot jar
    salsa   455 g
¼ cup sour cream   60 g
1 tablespoon flour   15 ml
3 tablespoons snipped
    fresh cilantro   45 ml
1 (8 ounce) package
    shredded 4-cheese
    blend   230 g

- Cut tortillas into 6 wedges. Place half of tortilla wedges in sprayed slow cooker.

- Layer chicken, corn and beans over tortillas in slow cooker.

- Combine salsa, sour cream, flour and cilantro in bowl and pour over corn and beans. Cover and cook on LOW for 3 to 4 hours.

- Place remaining tortilla wedges on baking sheet, bake for about 10 minutes at 250° (120° C) and set aside.

- When ready to serve, place baked tortilla wedges and cheese on top of each serving. Serves 6.

Tom Turkey Bake

1½ pounds turkey tenderloin	680 g
1 (6 ounce) package Oriental rice and vermicelli	170 g
1 (10 ounce) package frozen green peas, thawed	280 g
1 cup sliced celery	100 g
¼ cup (½ stick) butter, melted	60 g
1 (14 ounce) can chicken broth	400 g
1½ cups fresh broccoli florets	105 g

- Cut tenderloins into strips. Saute turkey strips in non-stick skillet until it is no longer pink.

- Combine turkey strips, rice-vermicelli mix with seasoning packet, peas, celery, butter, chicken broth and 1 cup (250 ml) water in large slow cooker and mix well.

- Cover and cook on LOW for 4 to 5 hours. Turn heat to HIGH setting, add broccoli and cook for an additional 20 minutes. Serves 6

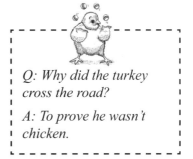

Q: Why did the turkey cross the road?

A: To prove he wasn't chicken.

Smoked-Turkey Sausage

This is a great recipe for leftover turkey.

2 cups cooked, cubed turkey	**280 g**
½ pound smoked turkey sausage	**230 g**
3 carrots, sliced	
1 onion, halved, sliced	
1 (15 ounce) can navy bean	**425 g**
1 (15 ounce) white lima beans	**425 g**
1 (8 ounce) can tomato sauce	**230 g**
1 teaspoon dried thyme	**5 ml**
¼ teaspoon ground allspice	**1 ml**

- Cut turkey sausage in ½-inch (1.2 cm) pieces. Combine all ingredients in sprayed slow cooker. Cover and cook on LOW for 4 to 5 hours. Serves 6.

Gobble-It-Up Turkey Loaf

2 pounds ground turkey	**910 g**
1 onion, very finely chopped	
½ red bell pepper, seeded, very finely chopped	
2 teaspoons minced garlic	**10 ml**
½ cup chili sauce	**135 g**
2 large eggs, beaten	
¾ cup Italian seasoned breadcrumbs	**90 g**
Salsa	

- Combine all ingredients plus 1 teaspoon (5 ml) salt and ½ teaspoon (2 ml) pepper in large bowl and mix well. Shape into round loaf and place in slow cooker.

- Cover and cook on LOW for 5 to 6 hours. Remove from cooker to serving plate and serve with salsa. Serves 8.

Turkey Sausage and Rice

1 pound turkey sausage	455 g
1 (6 ounce) box Rice-a-Roni®	170 g
2 (14 ounce) cans chicken broth	2 (400 g)
2 cups sliced celery	200 g
1 red bell pepper, julienned	
1 (15 ounce) can cut green beans, drained	425 g
⅓ cup slivered almonds, toasted	55 g

- Break up turkey sausage and brown in skillet. Place in sprayed 4 to 5-quart (4 to 5 L) slow cooker. Add rice, 1 cup (250 ml) water, chicken broth, celery, bell pepper and green beans and stir to mix.

- Cover and cook on LOW for 3 to 4 hours. When ready to serve, sprinkle almonds over top. Serves 8.

Turkey Spaghetti

2 pounds ground turkey	910 g
2 (10 ounce) cans tomato bisque soup	2 (280 g)
1 (14 ounce) can chicken broth	400 g
1 (15 ounce) can whole kernel corn, drained	425 g
1 (4 ounce) can sliced mushrooms, drained	115 g
¼ cup ketchup	70 g
2 (7 ounce) boxes ready-cut spaghetti	2 (200 g)

- Cook ground turkey in non-stick skillet and season with a little salt and pepper. Place cooked turkey in sprayed 5 to 6-quart (5 to 6 L) slow cooker.

- Combine soup, broth, corn, mushrooms and ketchup in bowl and stir to blend. Add spaghetti to slow cooker and pour soup mixture on top. Cover and cook on LOW for 5 to 7 hours or on HIGH for 3 hours. Serves 8.

Winter Dinner

1 pound chicken tenderloins	455 g
Olive oil	
1 pound Polish sausage	455 g
2 onions, chopped	
1 (28 ounce) can pork and	
beans with juice	795 g
1 (15 ounce) can ranch-style	
beans, drained	425 g
1 (15 ounce) can great	
northern beans	425 g
1 (15 ounce) can butter	
beans, drained	425 g
1 cup ketchup	270 g
1 cup packed brown sugar	220 g
1 tablespoon vinegar	15 ml
6 slices bacon, cooked,	
crumbled	

- Brown chicken slices in skillet with a little oil and place in large sprayed slow cooker.

- Cut sausage in 1-inch (2.5 cm) pieces and add to slow cooker.

- Combine onions, 4 cans beans, ketchup, brown sugar and vinegar in bowl, add to slow cooker and stir gently.

- Cover and cook on LOW for 7 to 8 hours or on HIGH for 3 hours 30 minutes to 4 hours. When ready to serve, sprinkle crumbled bacon over top. Serves 12.

Chicken, Alaska got its name because the locals wanted to honor the state bird, the Ptarmigan, by naming their town Ptarmigan, Alaska. But they couldn't spell Ptarmigan. However, they could spell chicken.

One Last Peep

Ingredient Equivalents

Convenience Foods to Keep on Hand

Index

Ingredient Equivalents

Food	Amount	Approximate Equivalent
Apples	1 pound fresh	3 medium 2¼ cups chopped 3 cups sliced
Bacon	1 slice, cooked	1 tablespoons crumbled
Bread	1 (1 pound) loaf	14 - 18 regular slices 7 cups crumbs
	1 slice	½ cup crumbs
Breadcrumbs	1 (8 ounce) package	2⅓ cups
Breadcrumbs, dry	1 cup	¾ cup cracker crumbs
Broccoli	1 pound fresh	2 cups chopped
Broth, chicken or beef	1 cup	1 bouillon cube 1 teaspoon granules in 1 cup boiling water
Butter	1 pound regular	4 sticks 2 cups
	1 stick	½ cup 8 tablespoons
	1 cup (4 ounces)	⅞ cup vegetable oil or shortening 1 cup margarine
Buttermilk	1 cup	1 tablespoon lemon juice or white vinegar plus milk to equal 1 cup (must stand for 10 minutes)
Celery	2 ribs	½ cup chopped
Cottage Cheese	1 cup	1 cup ricotta
Crackers	15 graham crackers	1 cup crumbs
	28 saltine crackers	1 cup crumbs

Food	Amount	Approximate Equivalent
Cream	½ pint light	1 cup
	½ pint whipping	1 cup; 2 cups whipped
	½ pint sour cream	1 cup
Cream Cheese	8 ounces	1 cup
Chicken	3 - 3½ pounds	3 cups cooked meat
	1 whole breast	1½ cups cooked, chopped
Chocolate	6 ounce chips	1 cup
Chocolate wafers	18 - 20 cookies	1 cup crumbs
Cornstarch	1 tablespoon	2 tablespoons flour
Cream, whipping	1 cup	4 ounces frozen whipped topping, thawed
Flour	1 cup sifted all-purpose	1 cup minus 2 tablespoons unsifted all-purpose
	1 cup sifted self-rising	1 cup sifted all-purpose flour plus 1½ teaspoons baking powder plus ⅛ teaspoon salt
Garlic	1 small clove	⅛ teaspoon garlic powder
Grits	1 pound	3 cups
Ham	½ pound boneless	1½ cups chopped
Herbs	1 tablespoon fresh	1 teaspoon dried
Honey	1 cup	1¼ cups granulated sugar plus ⅓ cup liquid in recipe
Ketchup	½ cup	½ cup tomato sauce plus 2 tablespoons sugar plus 1 tablespoon vinegar
Lemon juice	1 teaspoon	½ teaspoon vinegar
Lemons	4 - 6	1 cup juice
Limes	6 - 8	¾ cup juice
Macaroni	8 ounces	4 cups cooked
	1 cup	1¾ cups cooked

Food	Amount	Approximate Equivalent
Marshmallows	6 - 7 large	1 cup
	85 miniature	1 cup
Milk	1 quart	4 cups
Milk, evaporated	5 ounce can	⅔ cup
Mushrooms	½ pound fresh	1 (6 ounce) can, drained
	1 pound	5 cups sliced; 6 cups chopped
Mustard	1 tablespoon prepared	1 teaspoon dry
Oil	1 quart	4 cups
Onions	1 small	1 tablespoon instant minced ½ tablespoon onion powder
Onions, green	5 bulbs only	½ cup chopped
	5 with tops	1¾ cups chopped
Onions, white	4 medium	3½ cups chopped
Oreo	22 cookies	1½ cups crumbs
Peaches	4 medium	2½ cups chopped or sliced
Peanut Butter	18 ounce jar	1¾ cups
Pecans	1 pound shelled	4 cups chopped
Peppers, bell	2 large	2½ cups chopped 3 cups sliced
	1 medium	1 cup chopped
Potatoes, sweet	3 medium	4 cups chopped
Potatoes, white, red, russet	1 pound	4 cups chopped
Rice	1 cup regular	3 cups cooked
	1 cup instant	2 cups cooked
	1 cup brown	4 cups cooked
	1 cup wild	4 cups cooked

Food	Amount	Approximate Equivalent
Shortening	1 pound	2½ cups
Shrimp	1 pound shelled	2 cups cooked
	1 pound in shell	20 - 30 large 11 - 15 jumbo
Sour cream	1 cup	1 cup plain yogurt ¾ cup buttermilk 1 tablespoon lemon juice plus enough evaporated milk to equal 1 cup
Squash	1 pound summer	3 cups sliced
	1 pound winter	1 cup cooked, mashed
Strawberries	1 pint fresh	1½ cups sliced
	10 ounces frozen	1½ cups
Sugar	1 cup light brown	½ cup packed brown sugar plus ½ cup granulated sugar
	1 cup granulated	1¾ cups powdered sugar 1 cup packed brown sugar 1 cup superfine sugar
	1 pound granulated	2 cups
	1 pound powdered	3½ cups
	1 pound brown	2¼ cups packed
Tomatoes	3 medium	1½ cups chopped
Tomato juice	1 cup	½ cup tomato paste plus ½ cup water
Tomato sauce	1 cup	½ cup tomato paste plus ½ cup water
Vanilla wafers	22 cookies	1 cup crumbs
Wine	750 ml	3 cups
Yogurt	1 cup	1 cup buttermilk 1 cup milk plus 1 tablespoon lemon juice

Convenience Foods to Keep on Hand

Canned Savory Foods

Whole and chopped plum
   tomatoes
Beans
Vegetables such as
   corn, asparagus, and
   artichoke hearts
Tuna
Cooked ham
Sauces
Condensed and ready-
   to–heat soups
Peanut and other nut
   butters
Ready-made meals such
   as chili or baked beans;

Canned Sweet Foods

Pineapple
Pear rings and chunks
Peach halves or slices
Exotic fruits such as litchis
   and guavas
Fruit pie fillings
Applesauce
Fruit cocktail.

Dry Foods and Packaged Mixes

Sauce and gravy mixes
Dried vegetables and
   beans
Instant mashed potatoes
Pasta
Rice and rice mixes
Instant desserts
Dried milk
Gelatin
Bread
Pastry
Cake mixes
Bottled Foods
   and Preserves
Jams and jellies
Pesto
Olives
Sun-dried tomatoes
Antipasto.

Prepared Foods

Partly baked breads and
   pastries
Prepared ready-to-serve
   meals
Ready rice
Desserts.

Refrigerated Foods

Milk and cream
Prepared meals
Fresh pasta
Soups
Sweet and savory sauces
Fruit salad
Bag salads and dressings
Fresh pastry
Dips
Eggs

Frozen Savory Foods

Vegetables and stir-fry
   mixes
French fries
Cooked rice
Pizza bases
Prepared fish and shellfish
Meat and poultry

Frozen Sweet Foods

Fruits and seasonal soft-
   fruit mixes
Melon balls
Ices, sorbets, and iced
   desserts
Pastry
Pies
Cakes
Fruit juices
Whipped topping

Index

Frys, Grills and Sautes

G

H

I

J

K

L

M

N

O

P

T

Cookbooks Published by
Cookbook Resources, LLC
Bringing Family and Friends to the Table

*The Best of Cooking
with 3 Ingredients*

*The Ultimate Cooking
with 4 Ingredients*

*Easy Cooking
with 5 Ingredients*

*Healthy Cooking
with 4 Ingredients*

*Gourmet Cooking
with 5 Ingredients*

*4-Ingredient Recipes
for 30-Minute Meals*

*Essential 3-4-5
Ingredient Recipes*

The Best 1001 Short, Easy Recipes

1001 Fast Easy Recipes

1001 Community Recipes

*Busy Woman's
Quick & Easy Recipes*

*Busy Woman's
Slow Cooker Recipes*

Easy Slow Cooker Cookbook

Easy One-Dish Meals

Easy Potluck Recipes

Easy Casseroles

Easy Desserts

Sunday Night Suppers

Easy Church Suppers

365 Easy Meals

365 Easy Chicken Recipes

365 Easy Soups and Stews

365 Easy Vegetarian Recipes

Quick Fixes with Cake Mixes

*Kitchen Keepsakes/
More Kitchen Keepsakes*

Gifts for the Cookie Jar

*All New Gifts
for the Cookie Jar*

Muffins In A Jar

The Big Bake Sale Cookbook

*Classic Tex-Mex
and Texas Cooking*

Classic Southwest Cooking

Miss Sadie's Southern Cooking

Texas Longhorn Cookbook

Cookbook 25 Years

A Little Taste of Texas

A Little Taste of Texas II

*Trophy Hunters'
Wild Game Cookbook*

Recipe Keeper

*Leaving Home Cookbook
and Survival Guide*

*Classic Pennsylvania
Dutch Cooking*

Easy Diabetic Recipes

**_cookbook_
≋_resources_** ® LLC

www.cookbookresources.com

Your Ultimate Source for Easy Cookbooks

365 Easy
Chicken
Recipes

Quick, Easy Ways
to Cook Chicken

cookbook
resources LLC

www.cookbookresources.com